The Who

the Complete Guide *to their* Music

OMNIBUS PRESS

London/New York
Paris/Sydney/Copenhagen
Berlin/Madrid/Tokyo

Chris Charlesworth
& Ed Hanel

Cover and book designed by Chloë Alexander
Picture research by Sarah Bacon

ISBN: 1.84449.428.4
Order No: OP50281

Exclusive Distributors
Book Sales Limited
8/9 Frith Street,
London W1D 3JB, UK.

Music Sales Corporation
257 Park Avenue South,
New York, NY 10010, USA.

Music Sales Pty Limited,
120 Rothschild Avenue, Rosebery,
NSW 2018, Australia.

To the Music Trade only:
Music Sales Limited,
8/9, Frith Street,
London W1D 3JB, UK.

Every effort has been made to trace the copyright holders
of the photographs in this book but one or two were
unreachable. We would be grateful if the photographers
concerned would contact us.

Printed by: Mackays of Chatham plc, Chatham Kent.

A catalogue record for this book is available from the
British Library.

Visit Omnibus Press at http://www.musicsales.co.uk

Contents

INTRODUCTION

THE WHO'S FORTE WAS ALWAYS THE LIVE STAGE, BUT ALONG THE WAY THEY made some pretty decent records, as well as a few duffers. Like those rare bands who met as teenagers and managed to stay together through thick and thin, playing on stage became second nature to them – at least when they did it regularly – and on their best nights a sixth sense seemed to take over the tiller and lead them and their audiences towards a kind of rock heaven that most bands can only dream about.

For the first ten years of their career they probably played more live shows than any other band of their era but, relatively speaking, they were never prolific in the studio. In the Sixties, while The Beatles put out 10 studio albums and The Rolling Stones eight, The Who managed only four. Nowadays this miserly output is all too common among established acts, but back then top bands were expected to release an album a year *and* a few non-album singles while touring constantly, so even though The Who's output matched present day standards, they were still underachievers compared to their peers.

They didn't really speed up in the Seventies either, with just four more studio albums by the original band, a live set and a collection of unreleased outtakes. That said, there's still a total of just over 200 extant recorded songs credited to The Who, a substantial body of work by anybody's standards. Unfortunately there have been far too many unimaginative Who compilations along the way, which has resulted in only a small percentage of their total output being widely known. This is a great shame, because there's far more depth and enjoyment to be found in The Who's catalogue than 'My Generation', 'Pinball Wizard', 'Won't Get Fooled Again' and the half-dozen or so other Who classics that are endlessly recycled by most radio stations, especially in the US.

One of the reasons for The Who's relative underachievement in the studio was the court settlement awarded in 1966 to Shel Talmy who produced their first three singles and their entire first LP. After a bitter legal dispute, Talmy and The Who parted company but the American producer was awarded a substantial royalty on all their work up to and including *Who's Next*. The Who therefore found themselves in an ironic position: the more successful they became and the more records they sold, the more they enriched their worst enemy. It was financially crippling for them insofar as they never earned a just reward from record sales during the period when they sold most records. That's reason enough to limit your output and play live as often as possible (Talmy, of course, received zilch from live shows), but the whole awful business doubtless shaped the direction that The Who's career eventually took.

At first, like all their peers, The Who were a 'singles' band – there was no other type of band in 1965 and '66 – and most of their terrific early hits, none of which made any real impact in the US, weren't taken from concurrent albums as singles are today. Consequently, because this review of their work is album based rather than strictly chronological, some of their better-known early songs don't appear under analysis until the later chapter on compilations, many of them on *Meaty Beaty Big & Bouncy*.

In 1994 The Who received the box-set treatment with *30 Years Of Maximum R&B*, a well-received 4-CD retrospective of 79 mostly remastered tracks compiled by Chris Charlesworth. The strong response to that release justified a wholesale repackaging programme over the next few years for most of The Who's back catalogue, with the conspicuous exception of the *My Generation* album (Shel Talmy and The Who finally came to an agreement in 2002 – see entry).

The reissues involved upgraded CDs, usually supplemented with bonus tracks and informative 24-page booklets. The bonus tracks added a few surprises and alternative takes, while bringing up the running time for each CD from around 40 minutes to over an hour. (*Tommy* and *Quadrophenia* were the obvious exceptions based on their length as double albums.) Releases did not follow chronological order, with the series initially commencing in February 1995 with an expanded *Live At Leeds* (1970). The series then cherry picked its way through the band's standard catalogue, up to and including *It's Hard* (1982), inexplicably skipping over the *Meaty Beaty Big & Bouncy* compilation.

Even as audio buffs debated the merits of analogue vinyl vis a vis digital remixing and remastering, the technical development of new formats such as Special Audio Compact Discs (SACD), 5.1 Surround Stereo, and DVD Audio provided an opportunity for further, more recent, refinements. This has resulted in a second ongoing upgrade of The Who's albums, most recently highlighted by the SACD/CD hybrid release of *Tommy*, remastered by Pete Townshend himself from the original 8-track tapes. The addition of yet more material, such as the superb live recording from the *Lifehouse* project on the *Who's Next* Deluxe Edition, helps justify the purchase of yet more remastered editions. At least that is what we tell our patient spouses!

While the consolidation of record companies – MCA in the States and Polygram elsewhere merging under the Universal banner – has created worldwide marketing opportunities, this has resulted in yet more compilations but has destroyed the likelihood of any difference in domestic releases, previously a source of intense interest to hardcore Who collectors.

Thanks to Andy Neill, John Atkins, Gary & Melissa Hurley, and Andrew King for their help and insights into The Who's music. A special thanks to "whitefang" and the use of the discography on his excellent website: www.thewho.info. Finally, on behalf of Who fans everywhere, a special acknowledgement to David Swartz for his role in the eventual reissue of Shel Talmy's masters.

Several quotes have been taken from interviews with The Who over the years and from Dave Marsh's excellent Who biography *Before I Get Old*. Who fans seeking further information about the band should also check out *Anyway Anyhow Anywhere: The Complete Chronicle of The Who 1958-1978* by Andy Neill & Matt Kent (Friedman/Fairfax 2002), *Maximum R&B* by Richard Barnes (Plexus 1982), *Dear Boy: The Life Of Keith Moon* by Tony Fletcher (Omnibus Press 1998), and *The Who Concert File* by Joe McMichael and 'Irish' Jack Lyons (Omnibus Press 1997; updated 2004).

In the first issue of *Generations*, a fanzine produced by Phil Hopkins and John Atkins, the latter wrote that The Who were "loud, brash, hard, noisy, fast and exciting, but also subtle, complex, intelligent, imaginative, and profound."

We couldn't agree more.

Chris Charlesworth, September 1994
& Chris Charlesworth and Ed Hanel April 2004

N.B: Space has precluded listing every vinyl reissue. Since this effort is primarily focused on CD releases, the compilers have included the original UK and US album catalogue numbers and most of the CD issues and reissues.

All songs written by Pete Townshend unless otherwise stated. Additional songwriting credits ignored after the first reference.

My Generation

Original UK issue: Brunswick Records LAT 8616,
released December 1965; reissued Virgin V2179, October 1980.

IN THE CLOSING WEEKS OF **1964** THINGS LOOKED BLEAK FOR THE WHO.
No record company showed much interest in them, there was no money
in the kitty, and their lately elected managers, Kit Lambert and Chris Stamp,
were at their wits end. Indeed, if it wasn't for the friendship between their
secretary, Anya Butler, and an American ex-pat record producer presently
domiciled in London, well, who knows whether The Who's recording career
might ever have got off the ground in the first place.

Shel Talmy went to see The Who at a rehearsal hall in Shepherd's Bush
and liked what he saw. "You just listened to them for five minutes and you
knew these guys had something," he said. "Their energy, their attack –
which groups (in Britain) did not have then." Talmy promptly signed a
decidedly ungenerous one-off production deal with The Who's managers
to record the group, then took the tapes to American Decca, who would
release The Who's records in the UK on their subsidiary label, Brunswick. The
small print on that contract with Talmy's Orbit Music incorporated a crucial
four-year option, however, and it's no exaggeration to suggest that the
catastrophic economic consequences of this little clause would effectively
govern the way The Who's entire career developed, even to this day.

Blissfully unaware of the problems that lay ahead, The Who sailed into
Pye Studios, near Marble Arch, with Talmy calling the shots, and recorded 'I
Can't Explain', their first single as The Who, in November 1964. Coupled
with a 'trad. arranged' Talmy composition, 'Bald Headed Woman', on which
Jimmy Page played fuzz guitar, 'Explain' was released in the UK on January
15, 1965. It entered the chart at Number 47 and peaked at 28 before
prematurely dropping out. After a fortuitous spot on *Top Of The Pops*' 'Tip
For The Top' slot, 'Explain' re-entered the charts and climbed to Number 8.
Simultaneously The Who could be seen playing their now legendary
Tuesday night residency at London's Marquee Club.

Talmy was anxious to record a follow-up but in 1965 (and for some
time to come) The Who were a working band in the strict sense of the word.
Not having received an advance against future royalties (heaven forbid!),
the group were obliged to perform regularly in order to support
themselves. It was unusual for them to perform less than 20 shows a
month at this stage in their career.

Nevertheless, The Who managed to record 12 completed songs
(accompanied by session pianist Nicky Hopkins) at IBC, over three days (12-
14 April), including their second single 'Anyway Anyhow Anywhere', which

was probably recorded on the 13th. The Who also recorded various soul and US numbers that they were incorporating into their stage act, including Eddie Holland's 'Leaving Here' (which remained unreleased until the US-only *Who's Missing* compilation in 1985), Martha & The Vandellas' 'Heatwave' and 'Motoring' (both released on the follow-up, *Two's Missing* in 1987), and Paul Revere & The Raiders 'Louie Go Home' (first released on *Who's Missing* and previously recorded by Davie Jones & The King Bees as the B-side to their 1964 Vocalion single 'Liza Jane'; Davie Jones, of course, became David Bowie). For reasons lost to the passage of time, the title was revised to 'Lubie (Come Back Home)'. Other tracks recorded included covers of 'Daddy Rolling Stone' (chosen as the UK B-side for 'Anyway...'), Garnet Mimms' 'Anytime You Want Me' (the US B-side), Bo Diddley's 'I'm A Man', a healthy dose of James Brown ('I Don't Mind', 'Please Please Please' and 'Shout And Shimmy') and, finally, a Pete Townshend original, 'You're Going To Know Me' (aka 'Out In The Street').

It was the practice in those days to record an album quickly to cash in on a hit single, and debut albums invariably comprised those songs from a band's live repertoire with which they were most confident. That's what happened with The Beatles and The Rolling Stones, and it almost happened with The Who. In the event, Pete Townshend's rapid progress as a songwriter forestalled such plans, so much so that many of these tracks remained in the can for years and The Who's debut album, postponed until later in the year, ended up including nine Townshend originals.

It wasn't until October 13 that The Who saw the inside of IBC again, and this time they recorded two Townshend originals, 'The Kids Are Alright' and 'My Generation' during a midnight session, with Talmy producing. On November 10 and 12, 'It's Not True', 'A Legal Matter' (with vocals by Pete – he doesn't recall why), 'Much Too Much', 'La La La Lies', 'The Good's Gone', and an instrumental, 'The Ox', were cut. All of these recordings made the final cut, together with 'Out In The Street', 'I Don't Mind', 'Please Please Please' and 'I'm A Man' from the earlier April sessions.

Few albums have been so crunchingly influential. Scores of noisy bands that followed have cited The Who's début as their inspiration. Indeed, the interplay between Moon's crashing drums (this album demonstrates unequivocally that Moon was far and away the most imaginative and talented young drummer in England) and Entwistle's super speed trebly bass, Townshend's ringing chords and use of the guitar as a sonic tool rather than a melodic instrument, and Daltrey's truculent vocal attack, was quite unlike anything else around at the time. Special mention is due to Nicky Hopkins, the session pianist, who was brought in to help fill out The Who's sound but managed to sound like a fully paid-up member of the band, no mean achievement in a quartet as combative as The Who at this stage in their evolution. The whole thing made The Who's main competition, The Beatles and the Stones, sound very tame, albeit better disciplined... mainly because Talmy was attempting to record the group in the same explosive way that they performed on stage. However the band and Kit Lambert were disenchanted with Talmy because they didn't have any say in the recording process and claimed that engineer Glyn Johns did all the work!

My Generation was released in December 1965, featuring an iconic front sleeve, taken in October by Decca Records' photographer David Wedgbury at Surrey Docks in south east London, featuring an aerial view of the four members of The Who gazing skywards, a pose that other bands, Blondie, The Jam and The Undertones amongst them, copied in almost perfect pastiches years later. In the US, where American Decca released the album in April 1966, the title was changed to *The Who Sings My Generation*, and the risqué 'I'm A Man' was deleted in favour of 'Instant Party' (aka 'Circles'), another Townshend original that prominently featured Entwistle's French horn. In an attempt to jump on the British Invasion bandwagon, a different yet similarly iconic Wedgbury shot, featuring The Who with London's most famous clock tower, Big Ben, in the background was offered up for American consumption. Although many fans didn't grasp it at the time, the new cover was particularly appropriate in view of the 'Englishness' for which The Who would eventually become renowned in the States.

My Generation reached Number 5 in the UK charts but flopped in the US. Polydor, who would release The Who's recordings in the UK over the next two decades, didn't own the rights to the album, which went out of print in the UK within 12 months of its release. For years no company seemed inclined to reissue the album in Britain until, curiously, Virgin picked it up in 1980. (This issue had good sound quality but was pressed on inferior vinyl and appears to have been copied directly from the album, not from Talmy's master tapes. It disappeared at the end of its meagre print run.) Decca kept the US version available domestically throughout the Sixties and, when MCA reorganised in the early Seventies, *The Who Sings My Generation* was issued as a double budget package with the US-only *Magic Bus – The Who On Tour*. When MCA first issued the album on CD in the States in the early Eighties, the company was promptly criticised for the mastering job and a better version followed but with the same catalogue number.

In 1994, The Who's career defining 4-CD box set, *30 Years of Maximum R&B* was released. It was the hope of those involved that each track would be taken from original masters. Pete Townshend's tape library revealed everything that he had hung onto for three decades – everything except the Shel Talmy 3-track masters of all The Who songs he'd produced in 1965. Negotiations with Talmy broke down, evidently because MCA and Polydor were unable to reach an agreement regarding advances and royalties. The compilers were thus obliged to use Pete's inferior mono tape copies.

And that's how the situation seemed likely to remain until Talmy placed the original master tapes on auction website e-Bay in 2000 at a starting bid of $500,000. Chris Charlesworth heard about this unusual gesture through the Who grapevine and contacted Townshend who said he was not interested in paying for the tapes and neither were The Who collectively; nor were the Who's record labels, MCA and Polygram, soon to merge under the Universal Music banner. The problem was the asking price. As desirous as an updated *My Generation* appeared to fans, it seemed unlikely to recoup $500,000 in royalties at such a late date. Talmy could sell the tapes as an item of memorabilia but that did not cover publishing rights. The purchaser would own an expensive cache of tapes but would not be able to do much with them. It was clear that a mediator was needed, someone without an axe to grind who could bring both sides together.

Enter American Who collector David Swartz. At the prompting of Charlesworth, Swartz visited Talmy in Los Angeles and pointed out that his demands were unfeasible. David also explained that the tapes were a diminishing asset since The Who's fan base was not getting any larger (just older!). In years to come, the tapes' value would diminish further. This seems to have cleared the way. The deadlock was broken and a deal struck. Talmy reduced his price to something between $50,000 and $100,000, Townshend got in touch, and so did the record company MCA. Remixed by Talmy, *My Generation* found its way onto US record racks in late August 2003 as a pristine-sounding double CD, bolstered by copious bonus tracks. What was probably one of the most significant debut albums in rock'n'roll was once again available.

OUT IN THE STREET

A FLAMENCO-like guitar flourish in the style that Pete used on several early Who songs opens this spiky, jerked-up rocker that sets the stage for their uncompromising style of what was termed 'Maximum R & B' on the distinctive B&W poster advertising The Who's Marquee shows. On the circuit The Who began by playing R&B covers but with such musical brashness at their disposal the songs metamorphosed into a fairly brutal style of rock and 'Out In The Street' exemplifies this. Nothing to do with the Bruce Springsteen song of the same name, although Townshend's lyrics carry a similar message: Don't Mess With Me.

I DON'T MIND
(Brown)

SLOW, soulful blues seems at odds with the violent attack of songs like 'My Generation' but this is the material that Roger liked to sing. Although his pitching isn't perfect, the band creates just the right atmosphere – tense and moody throughout. There's a great little guitar flourish at the end of the solo.

THE GOOD'S GONE

THIS IS A cheerless, forbidding song, definitely the moodiest on the album, taken at a deliberate pace with Roger adopting an uncharacteristically deep voice. If The Who's intention was to create an air of menace, the band succeeded admirably. Hopkins' piano and Keith's drums duel away in the background.

LA LA LA LIES

AN ATTRACTIVE melody is given greater emphasis by Keith who restricts himself to just tom-toms on the verse and chorus, an unusual arrangement for the time. Only on the middle eight and solo is he allowed to crash his cymbals. Shel Talmy released this track as a single without The Who's consent and it might even have been a hit had it not been in competition with the far superior 'Happy Jack' in November 1966.

MUCH TOO MUCH

FAIRLY standard beat group fare for the period, enlivened – as ever – by Keith's drumming and Roger's loutish vocal delivery in which he rejects his girl for displaying feelings too deep for him to reciprocate, probably a common enough state of affairs for Daltrey at the time.

MY GENERATION

IF 'MY Generation' were the only record The Who had ever recorded, they would still deserve an honourable mention in any roll-call of rock. Their third single – *the* Mod anthem – 'My Generation' is arguably the best-known song in The Who's entire catalogue. Pete Townshend has often expressed regret at penning the memorable line, 'Hope I die before I get old,' but 'My Generation' remains the hardest hitting single released by any UK pop group in 1965.

'Generation' started life as a slow blues, not unlike the version that The Who would often play in concert during the Seventies. Kit Lambert suggested Pete speed things up. Just before it was released as a single in October – at the suggestion of co-manager Chris Stamp – Roger was fired from the band for his violent behaviour. He was quickly reinstated and

'Generation' leapt up the charts to No. 2. Its success undoubtedly saved Roger from life as a tearaway – and The Who from extinction.

It's a cataclysmic *tour de force*, from Roger's controversial stuttering vocals to John's punchy bass solo, from Pete's grungy two chord guitar riff to Keith's by now regular assault on the drums, and its rebellious stance was a perfect war cry for those under 20 who felt that the grown-up world just wasn't for them. As if the first two raging minutes weren't enough, The Who piled on the pressure with an upward key change and climax with a brutal wipe-out of distorted feedback and general mayhem.

The fact that 'The Carnival Is Over' by The Seekers kept 'My Generation' from reaching the top slot may have terminally affected Pete's attitude towards the singles charts – probably for the better in the long run. It barely charted in the US, reaching only 93.

THE KIDS ARE ALRIGHT

THE WHO offer up another Mod anthem, recorded at the same session as 'Generation'. Although nowhere near as brutal, 'The Kids Are Alright' is equally as haunting in different ways. Opening with a lovely chord flourish – by now a Who trademark – and based around Townshend's favourite jangling A and D chords, 'Kids' is as melodic as any track on the album, even Beatleish in concept, but again it's Keith's

enormous drumming that drives the song to its many crescendos. Perhaps the most impressive section in the whole piece is the guitar solo, more slashing chords that reach a stupendous clanging climax, all underpinned by Keith, giving Pete and Roger a launch pad into the final verse that all of Britain's serious up and coming guitarists must have envied.

A cloth-eared A&R man at US Decca edited out this powerful solo on the US version of the album. Not until the release of The Who's 4-CD box set was the unedited version officially made available there.

PLEASE PLEASE PLEASE
(Brown/Terry)

IN WHICH Roger emotes in true James Brown fashion and the band provides back-up staccato style. Actually, Roger squeezes everything he can from Brown's showstopper, grossly overdoing it in the process. Pete's lively but rambling blues solo provides some interesting moments and barely saves the song from floundering as typical early Sixties UK white boy posturing. This one might have worked live, but on record everyone seems to try too hard with disappointing results.

IT'S NOT TRUE

WITH A lighter touch than the rest of the album, 'It's Not

True' approaches the typical beat group sound of the Sixties, but with The Who's rhythm section pounding away, it's a far cry from Merseybeat. Keith, in particular, excels on an upbeat song in which Roger denies a variety of slanderous rumours about his shady past, most of which probably were true!

I'M A MAN
(McDaniel)

BO DIDDLEY'S lurching blues standard became an album highlight in the hands of The Who, with Roger's macho attack perfect for its strutting delivery. Pete wades into a lengthy solo complete with volume control feedback 'freakout' effects, all the while duelling with Nicky Hopkins' more tastefully played piano. Effectively, they turn the second half of the song into a fiery instrumental showcase.

'I'm A Man' did not appear on the US LP and is not on the original MCA CD. However, it does appear on the US album *Two's Missing* (see entry.)

A LEGAL MATTER

A NAGGING little riff underpins a song about divorce – hardly common material for pop songwriters in 1965 – which is given a keen edge by the knowledge that Roger was indeed suffering the slings and arrows of marital breakdown at this time. Perhaps that's why Pete sings lead over Nicky Hopkins piano. Clearly influenced by the Stones, especially 'The Last Time,' which it resembles in many respects, Decca chose to release 'A Legal Matter' as a single without The Who's consent, after band and label had parted company in March 1966, but it only reached Number 32. "It's a legal matter, baby" indeed sounds a clarion call for lawyers everywhere.

THE OX
(Townshend/Entwistle/Moon/ Hopkins)

THE CLOSING instrumental is a far cry from the kind of melodic efforts recorded by instrumental groups like The Shadows, The Ventures or, indeed, any instrumental band of the day. Keith's relentless tom-tom barrage carries the music throughout, but the featured instruments are Pete's abandoned guitar slashes and Nicky Hopkins' piano, with John's menacing bass acting as a counterpoint rumble from somewhere deep within. 'Waikiki Run' by The Surfaris is the logical touchstone for Keith, who always was a huge fan of surf music and its rolling drum style, but there the surfing allusion stops. 'The Ox' is actually a 12-bar blues but it has no real melody in the accepted sense of the term, just the bass riff, and a brutal onslaught which at times teeters on the edge of musical anarchy, at least for its time.

Pete: "In the studio it was possible – with a bit of frigging around – to get the sound and energy we had on stage, and this is the first Who record where we really caught that. Because this is an instrumental, what you get is the band, the sound of this tremendous machine working almost by itself, that incredible chemistry we had in The Who, and that we kept right up until Keith Moon dropped dead."

Listening to Keith here, it's a wonder he didn't drop dead from exhaustion after the take ended.

The Who Sings My Generation

US: Decca DL 4664 (mono), DL 74664 (stereo), released April 1966, re-issued MCA 2044; CD: MCA 31330, September 1988, then re-mastered.

THE ORIGINAL **US** RUNNING ORDER RAN AS FOLLOWS: **'OUT IN THE STREET',** 'I Don't Mind', 'The Good's Gone', 'La La La Lies', 'Much Too Much', 'My Generation', 'The Kids Are Alright (edited version)', 'Please, Please, Please', 'It's Not True', 'The Ox', 'A Legal Matter', 'Instant Party'.

'Instant Party' (aka 'Circles') played an integral role in the dispute between Shel Talmy and The Who. The band re-recorded a self-produced version of the song, initially correctly credited as 'Circles', for the B-side of 'Substitute', released in March 1966, and a different pressing (released simultaneously) using the title 'Instant Party', to get around Talmy's claim of ownership. Talmy enjoined The Who from using the song and released the original version of 'Circles' he had produced – confusingly re-titled 'Instant Party' – as the B-side to 'A Legal Matter' and on the first US album, as if to re-emphasise his ownership of the song. Thus, 'Instant Party' is how early Who fans knew 'Circles'.

Frankly, Talmy's version sounds the better of the two, hardly surprising in view of his production experience at the time compared with that of the band and Kit Lambert. John's French horn is mixed up front and creates a disturbing aura missing from the Who-produced version.

My Generation

(Deluxe Edition)

CD: US MCA 088 112 926-2, August 2002, later SACD MCA 088 113 182-2;
UK Polydor 112 926-2, October 2002

THE HOLY GRAIL! AS MUCH AS THE WHO WANTED TO DISASSOCIATE themselves from their debut album because of the legal situation with Shel Talmy, this release is a vivid demonstration of a band and a producer who together created magic. For the reasons outlined below, this Deluxe Edition is not a faithful reproduction of the original album released in 1965/1966. It is, however, an aural delight that demands attention, and merits repeated playing.

Disc 1 opens with the songs in the same running order as the original UK album and while the re-mixed stereo was aurally impressive, it was not quite the same album released in 1965. Most listeners received a rude shock on hearing 'My Generation' and 'A Legal Matter'. Additional guitar overdubs, added in the final mixing stages, were absent from Talmy's masters. The mono versions of both songs were included as bonus tracks on the second disc to forestall complaints. Also missing were double-tracked lead and backing vocals, most noticeable on 'La La La Lies' and 'The Kids Are Alright'.

Also, the version of 'The Ox' has a proper ending instead of fading ten seconds early as per the original (a fact not credited on the sleeve and in the accompanying liner notes). The listener is sitting in the studio with the musicians on this remixed version, and we defy anyone who professes to love rock'n'roll to feel indifferent upon hearing it. Turn it up loud!

Bonus Tracks on CD 1

CIRCLES

THIS IS THE version that appeared on the B-side of the UK 'A Legal Matter' single and on the American album, *The Who Sings My Generation*, credited as 'Instant Party' (see above). For some reason, this new mix buries Entwistle's foghorn-like French horn just a little too far back into the mix.

I CAN'T EXPLAIN

THE FIRST single by The Who featured The Ivy League on backing vocals and is an unashamed attempt at copying the riff style of The Kinks who were also produced by Shel Talmy. This similarity to The Kinks aside, 'Explain' remains an explosive début, a song about the frustration of being unable to express yourself, not just to the girl of your dreams but, in a broader sense, to the world as a whole. Roger spits out the words in unresolved frustration while the band pound away, all of them aware that much depended on their performance. Special merit is due to Keith Moon, who announced his presence on the British pop scene with the kind of machine-gun drumming that was light years ahead of any of his peers.

In his Who biography *Before I Get Old*, Dave Marsh writes: "'I Can't Explain' is a slight song with a lyric on the edge of moony adolescent cliché, but as a recorded performance, it remains one of the outstanding documents of rock and roll. The sound is sharper, percussive, electric as a live wire. Voices ricochet off rim shots, bass lines throb beneath guitar static. Roles are reversed: Moon's drums take short, shotgun solos, functioning similarly to conventional lead guitar. Townshend's guitar punches out its notes as if he's playing drum fills. Daltrey slurs the vocals in striking contrast to both the taut accents of the instruments and the precise punctuation of the chorus... (he) transforms the character of the moonstruck kid to a glaring, hostile Mod whose inarticulate state is a sound of rage and frustration."

Roger: "The Kinks were certainly a huge influence on Pete and he wrote 'I Can't Explain', not as a direct copy, but certainly it's very derivative of Kinks' music. I felt a bit uncomfortable when I had to sing it."

Perhaps the best testament to 'Explain' is that throughout their career, The Who almost always opened their live shows with this song, occasionally alternating it with 'Substitute'. Is there any other band in the entire history of rock whose first single was so good, so timeless, that they could continue to use it as their opening number on stage for nearly 40 years?

'I Can't Explain' was released in the States in December 1964, four weeks before its UK release of January 15, 1965. The single struggled to reach 93 on the American charts in April 1965 while it became a Top 10 hit in the UK, eventually reaching the Number 8 spot the same month.

BALD HEADED WOMAN
(Trad arr: Shel Talmy)

A *VERY* short harmonica-based slow and moody blues song 'written' by Shel Talmy and used by him as the B-side of 'I Can't Explain', a common practice at the time that ensured that the producer would earn publishing royalties from sales if the A-side was a hit (which it became). Features Jimmy Page on fuzz lead guitar.

DADDY ROLLING STONE
(Otis Blackwell)

A FIERCE blues-soul workout with Roger and a live Who favourite.

Originally released as the UK B-side to 'Anyway Anyhow Anywhere' it was not officially available in the US until the *Two's Missing* album in 1985.

Deluxe Edition Disc 2

LEAVING HERE (ALTERNATE)*
(Holland/Dozier/Holland)

L IKE MANY of the covers included on this disc, this song was from The High Numbers/Who stage act, and was intended for inclusion on the first attempt at a debut Who album. Thanks to Townshend's compositional flair, that became unnecessary as the band began recording original material instead.

'Leaving Here' was originally a minor hit for Eddie Holland (of the Tamla hit writing partnership, Holland/Dozier/Holland) and features a curious pro-feminist lyric for the time. Though Roger's vocals sound edgy, the band play in a powerful, unrestrained manner, which would soon become their trademark.

See *Odds & Sods* bonus tracks for an alternate version and *Who's Missing* for a variant of this take.

LUBIE (COME BACK HOME)
(Revere/Lindsay)

U NSOPHISTICATED treatment of this derivative of 'Louie Go Home' by Paul Revere & The Raiders before The Who settled on the style they made their own. Omitted from the first LP in favour of Townshend originals.

SHOUT AND SHIMMY
(Brown)

W ITH THEIR ability to turn soul into rock at the drop of a drumstick, 'Shout And Shimmy' became a passionate live work out, the first in a series of drum vocal duels that reached its apotheosis in 'Young Man Blues'. This version, used as the UK B-side of 'My Generation', is energetic enough, but check out the live version on *The Kids Are Alright* on which Keith Moon is The Who, and the other three are mere sidemen.

(LOVE IS LIKE A) HEAT WAVE
(Holland/Dozier/Holland)

THE WHO played an aggressive version of this Martha & The Vandellas hit on stage and felt comfortable with it enough to re-record a version for *A Quick One* in August 1966. This 'original' version first appeared on *Two's Missing*.

MOTORING
(Holland/Dozier/Holland)

THE WHO again cover Martha Reeves & The Vandellas. It's not one of the band's better early efforts, but the playing is disciplined and towards the end there is another early example of the drum and vocal exchanges that Keith and Roger would eventually perfect.

ANYTIME YOU WANT ME
(Ragavoy/Mimms)

A SLOW SOUL ballad by Garnet Mimms & The Enchanters on which Roger tries to emulate the sound of John Lennon's Arthur Alexander imitations on The Beatles' early LPs. Simple, melodic and with a nice piano track from Nicky Hopkins, it features some early Entwistle and Townshend background vocals – "ooh, ooh" style – and was the B-side to 'Anyway Anyhow Anywhere' in the US.

ANYWAY ANYHOW ANYWHERE (ALTERNATE)**
(Townshend/Daltrey)

A N ALTERNATE vocal version of 'Anyway Anyhow Anywhere,' originally issued on a French EP in 1965. Roger stumbles over the vocal in places and John and Pete's "ooh-ooh" backing vocals are noticeably different. Apparently this was the original version, with the vocals on the take released as The Who's second single being re-recorded but not preserved. As a result, the Deluxe Edition makes this obscure version widely available for the first time. Later pressings corrected the incorrect title, 'Anyhow, Anywhere, Anyway' on the back cover but not in the enclosed booklet.

INSTANT PARTY MIXTURE*

THIS 'RUNAROUND Sue'/'Monster Mash'/doo-wop ditty was inspired by The Everly Brothers' 1962 album *Instant Party*. An historical curio – Talmy originally intended it as the B-side to 'Circles', what would have been The Who's fourth Brunswick single – it lacked all the aggression The Who represented and can now be regarded as a disposable oddity. That said, Townshend's 'Johnny B. Goode'-style lead guitar at the fade is interesting enough to wish Talmy hadn't faded the song prematurely.

I DON'T MIND
(FULL LENGTH VERSION)*
(Brown)

THE GOOD'S GONE
(FULL LENGTH VERSION)*

MY GENERATION
(INSTRUMENTAL VERSION)*

ANYTIME YOU WANT ME
(A CAPPELLA VERSION)*
(Ragavoy/Mimms)

ANYONE questioning Daltrey's early vocal abilities should take a listen to this soulful, vocals-only version.

A LEGAL MATTER

MY GENERATION

THE MONO mixes that retain the guitar overdubs lost during the original mixing process.

*Previously unreleased to 2003
** Previously unreleased in UK/US

A Quick One

Original UK issue: Reaction 593 002, released December 1966;
UK CD: Polydor 835 728-24, remastered Polydor 572 758-2, 1995
remastered stereo Polydor 589 800-2, April 2002

Happy Jack

US: Decca DL 4892 (mono), DL 74892 (stereo), released May 1967
CD: MCA MCAD-31331 entitled, *A Quick One (Happy Jack)*, remastered
MCAD-11267 entitled, *A Quick One*, remastered stereo MCACD-11267.

BY THE TIME THE WHO CAME TO RECORD THEIR SECOND ALBUM THEY WERE heading towards penury through smashing up expensive gear on stage and living like Lords off stage. Thanks to a publishing deal arranged by Chris Stamp each member of the group was encouraged to contribute at least two songs. In return the publisher would advance £500 to each member, a considerable sum in 1966.

Creatively speaking, it was an absurd idea, especially at a time when Pete Townshend was writing material of the calibre of 'Substitute' and 'I'm A Boy', and *A Quick One* suffers as a result – a ragbag of styles of variable quality, lacking cohesion and any real sense of purpose. Townshend's compositions are infinitely better than anything else on the album, especially 'So Sad About Us' and the second half of 'A Quick One (While He's Away)', though Entwistle turned in his first great Who song, 'Boris The Spider'. Even the most charitable of Who fans must have scratched their heads at Moon and Daltrey's contributions.

The album was recorded between August and November of 1966, mostly at IBC Studios and released in December in the UK where it made Number 4 in the LP chart. In America, it was re-titled *Happy Jack* after the Top 30 single that had been released Stateside in March '67. To make room for the hit single, the American album lost 'Heat Wave'. In any event, conservative elements at American Decca would probably have found *A Quick One* too risqué for an LP title.

The remastered 1996 CD added a number of bonus tracks, of which the most important were the tracks that made up the November 1966 *Ready Steady Who* EP. Although the original UK album was only released in mono, audiophiles had known stereo mixes existed for most of the tracks. These versions were eventually pieced together to produce the remastered stereo CD. ('See My Way' and the alternate 'Happy Jack' both remain in mono.) Confusingly, MCA used the same catalogue number for the mono and stereo CDs, which makes it impossible to distinguish between the two.

RUN RUN RUN

A HEAVY sounding guitar riff opens The Who's second LP, suggesting – wrongly, as it turns out – that what's upcoming is a replica of the group's incendiary live show. 'Run Run Run' is one of the album's better songs, bashed out with a driving Stones-like enthusiasm but it's a tad monotonous and not one of Pete's better compositions. There's whining feedback in the guitar solo, which is ahead of its time, but as an opener the song is a disappointment.

This song was first recorded by a band called The Cat (featuring Speedy Keen, later of Pete protégés Thunderclap Newman) which Pete produced for the Reaction label.

The stereo CD version runs about 10 seconds longer and has an alternate guitar track at the fade.

BORIS THE SPIDER
(Entwistle)

THE FIRST ever John Entwistle song to appear on a Who album sets the pattern for the kind of offbeat macabre material for which 'The Ox' would become notorious as the years went by. Having been ordered by Pete to write two songs, John did very little until the eve of the session when Pete asked him how he was getting on. "No problem," he replied. "How does it go?" asked Pete. "Like this," said John, humming the first few bars that came into his head. 'Boris' was the result.

Slightly discordant, as many of John's songs would be, 'Boris' has an abruptly descending chorus line and a sort of middle eight with the words 'creepy crawly' repeated in the kind of off-key falsetto voice that parents use to frighten young children. With John dropping to a *basso profundo* for the hook line, it proved a stage favourite and was the only song on the whole album to endure throughout The Who's live career, offering light relief in concerts crammed with Pete's weightier songs. Justifiably proud of this composition, John would wear his spider emblem around his neck at many Who performances.

I NEED YOU
(Moon)

DAFT LYRICS aside, Keith's vocal contribution to the album takes its harmonies directly from The Beatles and although it's about as lightweight as The Who ever got in their early days, Keith managed to inject a certain wistful poignancy into his earliest known composition. There's also some thunderous drumming and a mock country and western harpsichord solo played by John Entwistle.

WHISKEY MAN
(Entwistle)

JOHN'S second contribution, about an inveterate boozer, lacks the punch of 'Boris' and the wit, but retains the slightly slurred vocal – appropriately in this case – and slightly off-key pitching, perhaps brought on by the DTs, that became characteristic of John's writing and singing style.

HEAT WAVE
(Holland/Dozier/Holland)

THE WHO'S ability to turn R&B into rock was unique at the time and their second stab at Martha & The Vandellas' hit is probably the closest they ever came to capturing their 'Maximum R&B' style on record. This is tight and lively but a bit short, in comparison to the Shel Talmy-produced version, available on either *My Generation* Deluxe Edition or the *Two's Missing* compilation. There are noticeable differences between the mono and stereo versions during the fade.

COBWEBS AND STRANGE
(Moon)

KEITH'S second composition was an eccentric instrumental, featuring drums and a brass band of sorts, all clanging together to what sounds remarkably like a children's nursery rhyme theme. Slight but charming and typically Moon, who conveyed the melody to the rest of the band by whistling it. Unfortunately, Keith seems to have relied rather heavily on jazz drummer Tony Crombie for inspiration. Keith was whistling a track called 'Eastern Journey' from Crombie's 1960 LP *Man From Interpol*.

By all accounts the scene in the studio when this was recorded was as eccentric as the track itself, with Kit Lambert leading the band in circles while they played assorted brass and percussion instruments: Pete on bass drum, Roger on trombone, Keith on tuba and John – the only one really playing anything – on trumpet.

DON'T LOOK AWAY

LIGHTWEIGHT C&W-style pop with pleasant vocal harmonies, but a weak, unconvincing guitar solo and inane lyrics ("My head's in a lion's mouth, wants to eat me up") reveals an early throwaway.

SEE MY WAY
(Daltrey)

THE FIRST of only three solo compositional credits by Roger in the entire Who catalogue sounds like a pastiche of something Buddy Holly might have written early in his career, then rejected. The song was not recorded by The Who as a band; instead the track consists of Roger and Pete's demo at the latter's Soho home studio. Keith's drums were added to fill out the sound.

Roger: "Nothing would please me more than to be able to write songs but unfortunately I'm not a songwriter. Believe me, if anybody's tried, I have. I'm not a natural."

SO SAD ABOUT US

THE BEST song on the album, originally written for The Merseybeats, The Who's version is a power pop feast of ringing power chords and harmony vocals fired off at a terrific pace over one of Pete's catchiest early melodies. The whole band are on top form. Listen out for the lovely counterpoint guitar lines that thread their way into the chorus, and the staccato guitar solo around the basic melody riff. Of all the lyricists working at the time, only Townshend had no qualms about slipping in 'la-la-la's' without compunction whenever he felt like it. 'So Sad...' is full of them, and all the better for it, but it also features the great line: "But you can't switch off my loving like you can't switch off the sun".

A QUICK ONE WHILE HE'S AWAY

PETE'S first attempt at a rock opera was inspired, original, mildly amusing but rather clumsy. It would never have been written had the other members' own compositions not come up short, so Kit Lambert proposed as a solution that Pete write a mini-opera to fill up ten minutes at the end of side two. 'A Quick One' was certainly complex, moving through six specific sections, all with different melodies of their own, ranging from camp country & western to lush harmonies and all out power pop, with a touch of English music hall in between. There is also a rousing Who-like power chord climax with quite stunning vocal harmonies, especially John's falsetto.

The six themes are 'Her Man's Gone', 'Crying Town', 'We Have A Remedy', 'Ivor The Engine Driver', 'Soon Be Home' and 'You Are Forgiven'. Along the way the unnamed heroine pines for her absent lover, selects Ivor as a substitute, regrets her folly when her man returns, confesses her indiscretion, and is ultimately forgiven.

'A Quick One' has its flaws but it was ambitious, especially for its time, and pointed the way towards a future for The Who.

Bonus Tracks on Remixed CD:

BATMAN
(Neal Hefti)

RECORDED at IBC Studios, August 1966, and released on the *Ready* Steady Who! EP on November 11, 1966. A largely instrumental version of the theme from the popular *Batman* TV series, played with verve and competence but eminently forgettable. The Who opened their live sets with the song at the time. Neal Hefti, who wrote the *Batman* theme, was also an arranger for the Count Basie Orchestra.

BUCKET T
(Altfield/Christian/Torrence)

RECORDED at IBC Studios, October 1966. The first track on the *Ready Steady Who* EP was this stab at an unremarkable Jan & Dean car song featuring Keith on reasonably well pitched lead vocals with the others doing high falsetto backing. The Who's surf music influence came solely from Keith whose all-time favourite song was 'Don't Worry Baby' by The Beach Boys, which also had lyrics written by Roger Christian. Although 'Bucket T' was a surprise hit for The Who in Sweden of all places – blondes the world over must like surf music – it was rather slight and nowhere near as impressive as the much denser 'Disguises' which opened side two of the EP.

BARBARA ANN
(Fassert)

ANOTHER track recorded at IBC Studios in August 1966 and released on the *Ready Steady Who* EP, this was originally recorded by The Regents whose version reached Number 13 in the US charts in 1961. Further surrendering to Keith's fondness for surf music, The Who do their best with The Beach Boys' hit

(Number 2 in the US in January 1966 and Number 3 in the UK a month later), but try as they might it's hardly their forté, and Keith's vocals obviously can't match those of his Californian idols. The highlight is Pete's throwaway solo.

The stereo CD version has a count-in and extra backing vocals.

DISGUISES

RECORDED at Pye & IBC Studios during June and July 1966, and undoubtedly the best track on *Ready Steady Who*, 'Disguises' is a brief attempt by The Who to move in the psychedelic direction that The Beatles displayed on their *Rubber Soul* and *Revolver* LPs. The production is denser than any other Who record up to this time, with a guitar clanging like hammer against anvil, backward tapes, a macabre Entwistle horn solo, and the subject matter decidedly bizarre for what appears at first glance to be a love song.

The stereo CD version features different vocals on the fade which runs about 8 seconds longer.

DOCTOR, DOCTOR
(Entwistle)

RECORDED at Ryemuse Sound, London, April 7-9, 1967, and originally released as the B-side to 'Pictures Of Lily' on April 21, 1967. This is one of John's best ever Sixties songs with the composer singing a series of mildly amusing lines about his various illnesses in a very high-pitched voice to a catchy rock melody.

I'VE BEEN AWAY
(Entwistle)

THIS WAS recorded at Regent Sound, London, November 1966, and originally released as the B-side to the UK 'Happy Jack' on December 9, 1966. A most un-Who like C&W song which meanders along to little purpose with amusing lyrics about feuding brothers, jail terms, and vengeance. As lightweight as The Who ever got in the Sixties.

IN THE CITY
(Entwistle/Moon)

RECORDED at IBC Studios, July 1966 and originally released as the B-side to 'I'm A Boy' on August 26, 1966, this features Keith and John on their own surf-influenced composition. Bottom heavy but reasonably accurate Beach Boys pastiche. No relation to the Jam song and album of the same name.

HAPPY JACK
(Acoustic Version)

PETE PLAYS cello on this version of 'Happy Jack', recorded at IBC Studios, November 1966. The electric version reached Number 3 in the UK charts in January 1967, and was also the first record by The Who to make the US singles charts. This acoustic version, with an extra verse and bridge, was previously unreleased.

MAN WITH MONEY
(Everly/Everly)

RECORDED at IBC Studios, August 1966, this Everly Brothers' song was originally recorded for their *Beat 'N'Soul* album, released in August 1965. It also appeared on the B-side of the Everlys' single 'Love Is Strange' later that year, which is probably where The Who first heard it. Previously unreleased prior to 1995.

MY GENERATION/LAND OF HOPE AND GLORY
(Elgar)

THIS PREVIOUSLY unreleased, as of 1995, recording of 'My Generation' coupled with Elgar's rousing patriotic anthem was originally intended for inclusion on the *Ready Steady Who* TV special and spin-off EP. Keith Moon's snare drum sound has never been bettered. The urbane Kit Lambert, in the producer's chair at IBC, can be heard offering his opinion at the climax: "That's perfect."

The Who Sell Out

Original UK issue: Track 612 002 (mono) & Track 613 002 (stereo),
released December 1967; UK CD: Polydor 835 727-24, remixed Polydor
527 759-2, 1995. US: Decca DL 4950 (mono), DL 74950 (stereo) released
January 1968, CD: MCA MCAD-31332, remixed MCAD-11268, 1995

SOMETIME **BETWEEN 1967 AND 1968 THE WHO CEASED TO BE A POP GROUP** any longer and became, arguably, Britain's first ever *rock* band. It was a transition that few of their contemporaries were able to make, and the two likeliest contenders – The Beatles and The Rolling Stones – had problems making the shift which The Who did not have. The Beatles' enormous popularity meant that they were unable to perform live any longer – and muscular live performance was a pre-requisite of being a *rock* band – while the Stones were grounded through drug busts and Brian Jones' inability to cut it on stage. The Who, erstwhile bronze medalists behind The Beatles and the Stones in the Sixties Pop Olympiad, thus shot through the gap and for a brief shining moment – three years actually – became the greatest of Britain's rock bands, and certainly the best live act in the world.

They and Cream (who unlike The Who were formed for the purpose) pioneered the modern concept of rock performance and touring, ushering in an era that continues in far more sophisticated forms to the present day. After The Who's tours of this period, no longer would groups perform their hits in 20-minute sets and then retire. From now on they would be expected to perform for at least an hour and generally longer, and offer music from their LPs, performed loudly and in a manner that enhanced the original recordings, either through sheer volume or musical virtuosity or both. They would also be expected to improvise, to offer some form of liberating stage show and even to perform unrecorded material hitherto unheard by the audience.

All of this occurred following the release of *The Who Sell Out*, their pop-art masterpiece. Largely overlooked at the time but now regarded by many as an album on a par with *Sgt Pepper*, The Who, and Pete in particular, embrace outside influences like acid rock and surrealism with a pop sensibility that gives the songs a far surer touch than those on the previous two albums. Nevertheless, The Who sound like nobody else, partly because Keith had by now confirmed his position as the most expressive drummer in rock and John the most fluid bass guitarist, but mainly because of Pete's songwriting style and the way in which he, Roger, and John, sang harmony vocals together. The Who had a definite style of their own that might have been influenced by others but one that no one else has been able to better.

The songs on the first side of *The Who Sell Out* are linked together by spoof commercials; loving tributes or brilliant satires depending on which critic the reader wants to believe. In any event, the commercials are similar to those heard on pirate radio stations, and in many ways the album stands as a tribute to the pirates who plugged their singles and did so much to help The Who's career. Why this idea wasn't carried over to the second side is anybody's guess, especially as further recorded commercials, which could have appeared on side two, have since come to light. The eye-catching sleeve design also enforced the 'sell out' concept, with the members of the group 'promoting' a variety of commercial products: Roger sits in a tub of baked beans (he caught mild pneumonia sitting in the cold tub during the shoot), Pete uses an underarm deodorant, Keith applies spot cream, and John extols the virtues of a body building course.

For all its imagination *The Who Sell Out* reached only a disappointing Number 13 in the UK LP charts, and failed completely in the US despite the heavy touring schedule that the band were undertaking there. Because of the touring, the album was recorded variously in London, New York, Los Angeles, and there were even some unproductive sessions in Nashville.

The CD versions have used the stereo mixes of the tracks, with the mono mixes still officially unavailable.

ARMENIA CITY IN THE SKY
(Speedy Keene)

AFFABLE Speedy Keene was first the drummer and then guitarist and occasional songwriter for Thunderclap Newman, the band for whom Pete produced the Number 1 hit single 'Something In The Air' in 1969. Most fans probably thought Pete had written 'Armenia' anyway, so close is the style to his. This song, space-age grunge thirty years ahead of its time, is acid-tinged rock with a guitar solo enhanced by electronic whooping effects, backwards tapes and a dense sound quite unlike anything else on the album. Some confusion surrounds the identity of the singer, as it seemed too high for Roger and the unusual timbre rules out Pete and John, so the smart money was on Keith. However Daltrey recently confirmed it was himself and writer Speedy Keene - especially noticeable on the high chorus.

HEINZ BAKED BEANS
(Entwistle)

THE FIRST of several spoof commercials on *Sell Out* is devoted to the traditional English kids' teatime dish. Actually it's a virtual re-write of 'Cobwebs And Strange' from the second album with added vocals.

MARY ANNE WITH THE SHAKY HAND

PETE'S second great song about masturbation – the first was 'Pictures Of Lily' – or a tasteless ode to an afflicted unfortunate? Either way 'Mary Anne' is one of the stand-out tracks on *Sell Out* that could have been a single had Pete not been in the midst of writing a series of even better songs, which didn't appear on albums at that time.

'Mary Anne' opens with lovely acoustic chords, which get better as Roger attempts to explain why the heroine is preferable to Jean, Cindy and the other girls on the block. Again there's a lovely chorded solo with Pete stretching out the notes on his acoustic guitar.

Once again The Who are well ahead of the pack when it comes to subject material, but whatever the lyrics, 'Mary Anne' would have been a winner on the melody alone. An alternative take of 'Mary' featuring electric guitar instead of acoustic, appeared in the US as the B-side of the 'I Can See For Miles' single, and in the US 'Hand' became 'Hands'. This also featured Roger singing the word 'shaky' through a tremolo effect to create a truly s-h-a-k-y feel!

See CD Bonus Tracks below discussing other versions.

ODORONO

THE SECOND spoof advert, this time an extended ditty extolling the virtues of a deodorant. Incidentally, 'Mr Davidson' was probably inspired by Harold Davison, a well-known London booking agent from the time. The mono mix is noticeably different from the stereo mix.

TATTOO

A STRING OF lovely arpeggios opens one of Pete's finest 'rites of passage' songs, this one based around the spurious idea that tattoos make 'a man a man'. 'Tattoo' boasts a particularly attractive and mature melody, and couplets with unusually complex rhymes about two brothers who decide to get themselves tattooed, only to regret the decision after parental objections and personal contemplation.

This song became stage favourite in the late Sixties, usually prefaced by 'Fortune Teller', and The Who have often returned to it.

OUR LOVE WAS

PURE POP with the kind of cascading ethereal harmonies at which The Who were by now becoming most adept, space age guitar work and an unusual chorus which works up to a final upward key change. Another potential single had not Pete already had enough singles in his pocket to keep fans happy for years. Again, the mono version is a completely different mix from the stereo version, notably Pete's guitar track. In the US this song was entitled 'Our Love Was, Is'.

I CAN SEE FOR MILES

MANY FANS' choice as the best Who single ever, preceded here by a priceless advert for Rotosound strings (as used by Entwistle): "Hold your group together...with Rotosound Strings".

The Who never sounded more together than on this superbly crafted long-distance single. Psychedelic without being trippy, it strains at the leash but is held together by Pete's taut, sustained guitar phrases, Keith's immaculate drumming, particularly under the melody, and a crackling electric feel. The solo is a revelation: buzzing feedback, choppy chords and Keith at his very best. Pete's two over-dubbed guitar parts could never be replicated in concert, which is why The Who rarely performed this all-time favourite on stage until 1989.

The failure of 'I Can See For Miles' to become a significant hit single (it reached Number 10 in the UK and Number 9 in the US) was a profound disappointment for Pete. "To me that was the ultimate Who record and yet it didn't sell," said Pete at the time. "I spat in the eye of the British record buyer."

The fact that 'The Last Waltz', a saccharine ballad of appalling sentimentality by the wretched Engelbert Humperdinck, held the top spot top at the time can't have helped.

The remixed CD version doesn't flange the guitar solo from speaker to speaker as the original LP or the first CD version.

I CAN'T REACH YOU

PRECEDED by a 'dynamic tension' Charles Atlas spoof, 'I Can't Reach You' was another great pop rock song, this time with Pete on vocals, with flowing harmonies and a lovely chorus. It's slightly marred by Pete's uninspired guitar solo, but a fine example of The Who's mid-Sixties style. Like 'Glow Girl' (see *Odds & Sods*) 'I Can't Reach You' was originally conceived as an 'air-crash' song in which a survivor was unable to reach a dying loved one.

MEDAC
(Entwistle)

JOHN'S light-hearted, Gilbert & Sullivan-esque spoof commercial for spot cream. The track was re-titled 'Spotted Henry' in the States.

RELAX

ACID ROCK *à la* early Pink Floyd, not The Who's natural territory, especially as the song is organ based, but the dense sound they achieve soars to great heights of psychedelia during the central instrumental passage. Pete Townshend was no stranger to the UFO Club in London's Tottenham

Court Road where the Syd Barrett-led Pink Floyd were regulars; indeed, Pete's future wife Karen Astley designed UFO posters at the time.

SILAS STINGY
(Entwistle)

AN ATTRACTIVE but still sinister little pop ditty about a miser sung more tunefully than most Entwistle pieces and featuring a novel churchlike organ in the background. This is appropriate for its precisely arranged choral exchanges. Veers towards a novelty, but Abba certainly borrowed the 'Money, Money, Money' line in their song of the same name.

SUNRISE

VIRTUALLY a Townshend solo piece, the first of many that would appear throughout The Who's catalogue, 'Sunrise' finds Pete in romantic mood, picking on acoustic guitar and singing a beautiful, high-pitched melody well beyond Roger's range. Even more than 'Behind Blues Eyes' from Who's Next, this is the closest The Who got to recording a ballad. "You take away the breath I was saving for sunrise," indeed.

Pete: "This one utilises quite a lot of chords picked up from Mickey Baker's Jazz Guitar tutors. They come in two parts, show all complex chords as box diagrams and will teach you more in an hour about jazz guitar than you will ever learn elsewhere."

RAEL

THE CHORD progression in the second half of 'Rael' is best known for its more carefully balanced appearance as a central theme of Tommy, where it becomes the instrumental passage in both 'Sparks' and the longer 'Underture'. On its first outing here, it forms the climax to Pete's second mini-opera, a more melodic, compact and altogether more balanced affair than 'A Quick One'. Although no narrative is evident from the lyrics, 'Rael' has a slightly ethereal, unearthly feel and its musical components – including some lovely high harmony singing – slot together in the same manner that Pete adopted in Tommy. Here, the famous 'Sparks' riff is emphasised by a deep, echoey, crashing sound, rather like the amplified noise of a squash ball smashing into a wall but more likely to be Pete experimenting with the reverb control on his amp.

It's been suggested that 'Rael' is an abbreviation for Israel, that the 'Red Chins 'referred to are Red Chinese and that the song is politically motivated. Either way 'Rael' is definitely a place, as the coda ('Rael 2') first released on The Who's 4-CD box set (see below), makes clear. Pete has written that a portion of the plot concerned the Chinese crushing established religions as their expanding population eventually takes over the whole world. But interpretations are meaningless as Pete himself admitted. "No-one will ever know what it means," he said. "It has been squeezed up too tightly to make sense."

Bonus Tracks on Remixed CD:

RAEL 2

THIS DIRGE-like coda to 'Rael' was originally recording produced by Kit Lambert at Talentmasters Studio, New York in August 1967. Also released on *30 Years Of Maximum R&B* in 1994.

TOP GEAR

A JINGLE recorded for the Who's appearance on the eponymous BBC radio show. Recorded at De Lane Lea Studios, October 10, 1967.

GLITTERING GIRL

A LIGHT pop song produced by Kit Lambert at De Lane Lea, circa March, 1967. Previously unreleased prior to 1995.

COKE 2

ONE OF two unused jingles for the Coca Cola company, recorded circa April 1967.

MELANCHOLIA

ORIGINALLY produced by Kit Lambert at Advision Studios, London, on May 29, 1968, 'Melancholia' is a curiously cold, cheerless but nevertheless powerful song taken at a slow, forced tempo that contrasts markedly with the style of music The Who were otherwise producing at the time. Also released on *30 Years Of Maximum R&B*.

BAG O'NAILS

"LOON at the Bag O'Nails" chirp Moon and Entwistle in a brief ode to a popular Swinging London nightclub. Recorded at De Lane Lea, October 1967.

SOMEONE'S COMING
(Entwistle)

THIS Entwistle song was produced by Kit Lambert at CBS Studios, London, May 1967 with brass arrangements recorded at Bradley's Barn, Nashville, on August 17, 1967, and first released in the UK as the B-side of 'I Can See For Miles'. Mexican trumpets herald Roger's first ever stab at a song written by John, this one a mildly-diverting but essentially lightweight pop song with lyrics in the 'Wake Up Little Suzie' mode. John wrote this about secretly seeing his then girl friend, Alison Wise, later his first wife and also the object of John's wit in 'My Wife' (from *Who's Next*).

JOHN MASON'S CARS (REHEARSAL)

IT'S BEEN suggested that John and Keith produced this jingle in the hope that after playing it to John Mason, the owner of an Ealing car showroom, he would offer them a free Bentley or two. Well, it worked with Rotosound Strings and even Premier Drums! Recorded at De Lane Lea, October 1967.

JAGUAR

ORIGINAL recording produced by Kit Lambert, either at De Lane Lea or IBC Studios, London, October 1967. Astonishing drums lead into one of the heaviest tracks The Who ever recorded. The vocals may have been added as an afterthought, for its the instrumental work, like that on 'The Ox', that carries a song whose lyrics could be influenced by either the car or the animal.

Also released in an edited version on *30 Years Of Maximum R&B*.

JOHN MASON'S CARS (REPRISE)

EARLY MORNING COLD TAXI
(Daltrey/Langston)

'TAXI' is a straight pop song written by Roger and Who roadie Dave 'Cyrano' Langston and is definitely Roger's best composition in The Who's catalogue.

It remained unreleased until it was included on *30 Years Of Maximum R&B*.

COKE 1 (SEE COKE 2 FOR DETAILS)

HALL OF THE MOUNTAIN KING
(Greig)

PREVIOUSLY unreleased prior to 1995, this instrumental, whose theme is borrowed from Greig's *Peer Gynt* Suite, was originally recorded by various UK based instrumental bands in the early Sixties.

RADIO ONE (BORIS MIX)

ANOTHER jingle used for the BBC *Top Gear* session. Recorded De Lane Lea on October 10, 1967.

John, Keith, Pete and Roger (seated), pictured in May 1965, the month
'Anyway Anyhow Anywhere' was released.

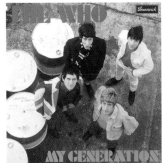

The mod's favourite band in the West End of London, and their debut album *My Generation* (1965) which disappeared from the shelves in the UK within a year of its release and only became readily available again on CD in 2002.

On the set of *Ready, Steady, Go!*, December 3, 1965, rehearsing 'My Generation'. Later that same night they played their final show at the Goldhawk in Shepherd's Bush.

On the streets of London's Chinatown in the summer of 1966, with Keith
supplying the refreshments and Pete seeking to blend in
with the natives.

Roger spent his advance from the *Quick One* album (inset, 1966) on a
new car, a sporty Volvo which was utilised for this photo opportunity
at London's Chelsea Barracks, November 12, 1966.

Backstage at *Top Of The Pops* in April 1967, when they performed 'Pictures Of Lily'.

November 2, 1967: Keith shows off his 'Pictures Of Lily' drum kit on *Top Of The Pops* (left) while Pete opts for the leather look too. That night they plugged 'I Can See For Miles'.

The Who Sell Out (1967): Roger caught mild pneumonia from having to sit in a tub of cold baked beans while the shoot was set up.

Tommy, the 1969 album that turned The Who into overnight superstars seven years after Roger, Pete and John first performed together.

The Who Live At Leeds (1970). US fans unfamiliar with the northern UK city were led to believe that The Who lived at Leeds.

Driving south towards Leicester on July 4, 1971, The Who spotted a slap heap just outside Sheffield and demanded a 'call of nature' stop. Photographer Ethan Russell, who was travelling with them, snapped this shot which became the cover of their classic *Who's Next* album (1971).

July 14, 1971: John, Keith, Pete and Roger pose for cameras in the grounds of Tara House, Keith's extravagant new home on the outskirts of Chertsey. It was the occasion of Keith's housewarming and doubled up as a launch party for *Who's Next*.

Roger on stage at London's Rainbow Theatre, December 8, 1972, rehearsing for the orchestral performance of *Tommy*.

GIRL'S EYES
(Moon)

THERE *was* a soft, sentimental side to Keith Moon, as this outtake demonstrates. After a typically Moon-like false start, it's a psychedelic folk-song, of sorts, that could have been written by Donovan, or even Syd Barrett. Gentle acoustic strumming shuffles things along and Pete closes the proceedings with what was probably the first and only take of his Spanish guitar-style soloing. Utterly charming. First released on *30 Years Of Maximum R&B*.

ODORONO (FINAL CHORUS)

THIS WAS the original final chorus, which was chopped off the *Sell Out* edit.

MARY ANNE WITH THE SHAKY HAND (ALTERNATIVE VERSION)

THERE ARE now four versions of 'Mary Anne' in circulation. The first appeared on *The Who Sell Out* LP and the second as the B-side of the 'I Can See For Miles' US single. A third version appeared on the upgraded *Odds & Sods* CD. This "fourth" recording was produced by Kit Lambert at Columbia Studios, New York, on August 17, 1967. The liner notes for the remixed CDs incorrectly assert that this electric version is the 'Mary Anne' that first appeared as the B-side of the US single. To the delight of fans everywhere, this was a previously unknown version instead. The US B-side may be found on *Rarities Vol 1*.

GLOW GIRL

THE LATEST recording to appear as a bonus track on *Sell Out*, this was produced by Lambert at De Lane Lea Studios, London, in January 1968, and first released on the album *Odds & Sods* in October, 1974. It was a precursor to *Tommy*, insofar as the closing lines introduce a Tommy melody, and seems to have been written about the contents of a girls' luggage on a plane about to crash.

In Pete's notes that accompanied *Odds & Sods*, he wrote: "It's a rock and roll airplane crash song with a real Pop Art plane crash and a happy reincarnation ending... I rarely leave any good idea unused, 'Rael' themes crop up in *Tommy* and so do the last lines of this."

TRACK RECORDS

KEITH AND John chanting "Track Records", recorded down a phoneline from the pub near to De Lane Lea Studios! It was then distorted to sound like an old scratched gramophone for the run-off groove on the original UK album pressings. Note how the Goons-like voices change "Track Records" to "Cracked Records".

Tommy

Original UK issue Track 613013/4; released May 1969:
UK CD: Polydor 800 077-2, remixed Polydor 531 043-2, 1996.
Deluxe Edition SACD hybrid Polydor 9861011, 2004
US: Decca DXSW 7205; CD: MCA MCAD-10005 (2 discs), MFSL UDCD 533
(1 disc), MCA MCAD-10801 (1 disc); remixed MCAD-11417, 1996.
Deluxe Edition SACD hybrid Geffen B0001386-36, 2003

THE WHO MADE *TOMMY* AND *TOMMY* MADE THE WHO. THAT'S THE POPULAR conception of the 'rock opera' that turned them into superstars and millionaires within the space of 12 months. There is no doubt that *Tommy* rescued The Who from financial ruin, developing eventually into a movie and a Broadway-style musical staged around the globe, but it proved also to be a weight around the band's neck. Although *Quadrophenia* was a more complex work on which the writing, playing, singing and production was superior in every way, it is *Tommy* for which The Who will be remembered above all else, save perhaps for 'My Generation'.

Recorded with Kit Lambert waving the baton back at London's IBC Studios between September 1968 and March 1969, *Tommy* brought together all of Pete's influences and aspirations in one great collage of ideas and ideals. *Tommy* is a Messiah figure elevated despite enormous disabilities to an otherworldly loftiness, brought down by reality and, finally, turned into a rock superstar-style deity. That's one view, the one that explains why Meher Baba, the Indian spiritual figure to whom Pete had lately become attracted, is credited as avatar. The other view is that *Tommy* is simply great rock music, almost 90 minutes worth, in which the form is explored every which way with extraordinary precision and timing and thus becomes a text book on riffing, rock harmonics, interlocking rhythms, electric and acoustic guitar backing, bass fluidity, vocal harmonies and every other skill with which a premier league rock band ought to be equipped. There is an almost mathematical precision to *Tommy* in the way that musical motifs – the 'Pinball' intro, the 'See Me, Feel Me' chorus, the 'Underture'/'Sparks' dynamics, the 'Go To The Mirror' riff – are introduced in the overture, then repeated at various moments throughout. Because these motifs crop up repeatedly in this manner, *Tommy* becomes much easier to assimilate on first listening than a double album of non-interconnected songs.

Pete and his friend Richard Barnes produced a whole book on *Tommy* in 1977 to attempt to explain it all, and on stage *Tommy* took on a whole other dimension – that's where it *really* became great – but it's The Who's recorded version that is the essence and cornerstone of the whole *Tommy* mythos. The original album, opulently packaged in a beautifully designed, surreal, triple-gatefold sleeve complete with libretto, was – by current standards – poorly produced in the studio and sounds very flat compared to certain other records in The Who's catalogue. The subsequent single CD version on which every song had been remastered was an improvement and features the cover originally intended for the album. The definitive version to own is obviously the recent SACD hybrid release. Heard in proper studio 5.1 surround stereo, *Tommy* becomes a sonic *tour de force* that has to be heard to be believed.

The Who's first official performance of *Tommy* was at a press preview at Ronnie Scott's Jazz Club in London on May 1, 1969, the same month the original double album was released. (The Who had actually tried out extended portions of *Tommy* at a few low-key shows prior to this 'official premiere'.) The final *Tommy* performance, until their 25th Anniversary reunion tour in 1989, was at London's Roundhouse on December 20, 1970, when they dedicated it to their support act, an upcoming singer-songwriter pianist called Elton John. In between, The Who dragged *Tommy* across Europe and America, performing it over 160 times. "Assemble the musicians," Pete would say as the band geared itself for 'Thomas', as he liked to call it. Keith would tap the rim of his snare like a conductor would tap his baton on a music stand. "Stop laughing," he'd yell from behind his drums. "This is serious. It's a fucking opera, ain't it?"

And off they'd go, crashing into the 'Overture' and sticking at it until the final verse of 'Listening To You', the coda from 'We're Not Gonna Take it', an hour and 15 minutes or so later. It was a marathon performance, something never attempted by any rock band before or since, and those fans who caught the opera in its glorious prime were indeed fortunate. Over the years *Tommy* would become abridged, with certain songs left out – 'Welcome', John's 'Cousin Kevin' and the lengthy 'Underture' were never played and 'Sally Simpson' generally got the chop too – until, by 1971, only the 'Overture', 'Amazing Journey', 'Sparks' (which, with its layered dynamics, sudden octave drops, and multiple rising crescendos, always brought audiences to their feet mid-way into the piece), 'Pinball Wizard' and the so-called 'See Me, Feel Me' climax remained.

Though Pete's development of the realms of rock opera often brought charges of pretension, The Who always maintained a slightly picaresque sense of humour when they performed *Tommy* live. This was certainly present during Keith's two vocal contributions, 'Fiddle About' and '*Tommy*'s Holiday Camp'. No one quite revelled in the role of a pervert quite like Moonie, as seen in his subsequent appearance as Uncle Ernie in Ken Russell's movie of *Tommy* (1975).

Pete has recalled that during a *Tommy* performance at The Kinetic

Playground, Chicago, on May 29, 1969, the audience – who'd had little opportunity to hear the album and therefore familiarise themselves with the music – rose at one point and remained standing, simply grooving away to the music. The band exchanged glances amongst themselves, realising there and then that they had created something very special. By the time *Tommy* reached its climax no-one was sitting down. And when the bright lights were switched on during the pummeling finish, The Who's auditoria became giant cathedrals in which, briefly, preachers and congregation were united in a massed celebration of rock music as the force for unification that Pete Townshend truly believed it was meant to be.

Despite the perfect timing – its mystical themes were ideal for 1969 – and the general hullabaloo surrounding its release, *Tommy* stalled at Number 2 in the UK charts. In America it eventually reached Number 4 upon re-entering the charts. Overall, it re-entered the *Billboard* charts several times for a total of 126 weeks, far longer than any other Who album.

Tommy was not the first album to be classified as a 'rock opera.' (It doesn't even really qualify as opera, the way that term is traditionally defined.) The Pretty Things had released *S. F. Sorrow* the previous year as just one of several contenders for the title, but arguably *Tommy* remains the best example of the genre.

OVERTURE

A PROPER opera needs a proper overture and like all overtures this one contains a well arranged mixed bag of instrumental snatches of the songs that will follow, most of them linked together by the rumbling, bass-heavy 'Go To The Mirror' riff. The guitar parts are played on Pete's acoustic Gibson J200, which sets a mood for the entire work, but John's French horn adds interesting melodic touches and, as ever, the choral work and drums are quite superb. The best moment in the overture comes towards the end when an organ arrives to pound out the 'Listening To You' melody from the 'See Me,

Feel Me' excerpt. At the close Pete is left strumming alone for a segue into...

IT'S A BOY

TOMMY'S birth, a brief introductory piece sung in a high register by Pete, followed by some impressive acoustic guitar work, leading into...

1921

THE FIRST melodic track, sung again by Pete who wrote several beautiful ballads for *Tommy*. This is one of them, although the song itself is intercut with a harsher refrain in which Tommy's parents urge their young son to forget the murder he's just witnessed from the reflection in the mirror... with disastrous consequences. Without this section, '1921' could have become a potential hit. In the US '1921' was titled 'You Didn't Hear It'.

AMAZING JOURNEY

THE FIRST great rock song on the album and a track which was a cornerstone for the whole *Tommy* project, it contrasts Keith's 'lead-the-way' drums with the lighter timbre that Roger adopted for most of *Tommy*. With backwards tapes to emphasise the state of Tommy's unbalanced mind, 'Amazing Journey' was one of many *Tommy* songs that came to life on stage and it segues directly into...

SPARKS

THE FIRST instrumental track, a deep-rooted, rumbling riff, endlessly repeated until, coming up for air, it slides into the better known 'Rael' melody that is explored in greater depth during 'Underture'. On stage 'Sparks' became a *pièce de résistance* of ensemble Who playing, with the band reaching higher and higher towards those block chord climaxes that defined their style. Here, they adopt a far lighter approach.

EYESIGHT FOR THE BLIND (THE HAWKER)
(Sonny Boy Williamson)

THE ONLY non-Who original song on *Tommy* is this brief excursion (which is referred to as 'The Hawker' in the libretto) into a blues by Sonny Boy Williamson II, also covered, jazz-style, by Pete's musical hero, Mose Allison. The heaviest number so far, it includes several references to Tommy's handicaps, thus helping to further the plot and sounding for all the world as if Pete wrote it himself.

In the Seventies, vinyl reissues of the album began using a version of this track with an alternate vocal. The early CD releases continued to do so as well. The MFSL 'Gold' and remastered CDs have reverted to the original.

CHRISTMAS

'CHRISTMAS', with its nagging, slightly off-key background vocal, is the first really Who-like song on *Tommy*, upbeat and slightly unnerving. At its heart is the first reference to the 'See Me, Feel Me' motif.

COUSIN KEVIN
(Entwistle)

JOHN'S FIRST *Tommy* song suits his offbeat, macabre style, telling the tale of Tommy's encounter with his evil cousin Kevin, the school bully, who does unspeakable things to the unfortunate boy. John's vocal is in a very high key, supposedly done deliberately so Roger couldn't sing it!

THE ACID QUEEN

A NOTHER *Tommy* highlight, 'The Acid Queen' features Pete on vocals for what appears to be an overtly drug oriented song with strong rock melodies and an infectious hook, but there's more to it than meets the eye...

Pete: "The song's not just about acid; it's the whole drug thing, the drink thing, the sex thing wrapped into one big ball. It's about how you get it laid on you that if you haven't fucked forty birds, taken sixty trips, drunk fourteen pints or whatever... society – people – force it on you. She represents this force."

UNDERTURE

A VERY lengthy instrumental version of the melody from 'Rael' (from *The Who Sell Out*) played on acoustic guitar in its entirety, with Keith's pounding drums hustling it along. Indeed, Keith's sense of timing throughout makes this a work that defines his skills as a drummer. Wrote Tony Fletcher in *Dear Boy*, his definitive biography of Moon: "... Moon offers up a series of emotive crescendos or otherwise doubles up on the guitar's complex rhythms, and then overdubs the whole with

grandiose symphonic timpani that take the number into another dimension. His rat-a-tat rolls on the snare that underscore Townshend's suspended fourth chords halfway through are potentially the definitive example of the pair's innate musical understanding; confident and unforced, they lift an already thrilling composition higher still."

DO YOU THINK IT'S ALRIGHT

A QUICK vocal link into...

FIDDLE ABOUT
(Entwistle)

W HICH TELLS of Tommy's dreadful experiences at the hands of the family pervert and was an ideal vehicle for John's warped sense of humour. The wicked Uncle Ernie, presumably Kevin's dad, would eventually become synonymous with Keith's more depraved caricatures. Here it's a mildly amusing comical song, which, like 'Cousin Kevin', John's other contribution to *Tommy*, sounds a bit out of place among Pete's songs. John sang this live when *Tommy* was first aired on stage in its entirety but Keith later took over and reveled in its malevolence.

PINBALL WIZARD

PETE Townshend has often been called the greatest rhythm guitarist in rock, and no better evidence survives than the furious acoustic strumming which underpins 'Pinball Wizard', the best known song from *Tommy* and another serious contender for the best Who song of all time.

From the opening minor chords to the upward key change near the end, 'Pinball' is a rock *tour de force*, brimful of ideas, power chords, great lyrics and tight ensemble playing. The concept of a deaf, dumb and blind pinball champion might stretch the imagination but anything can be forgiven in the context of this song.

The idea of a pinball Messiah came from Nik Cohn, the UK's most perceptive rock writer in the Sixties and a personal friend of Pete and Kit Lambert, whose girlfriend at the time really was a pinball queen. By 1969, Cohn was writing rock reviews for the *New York Times* and there seems little doubt that he was strong-armed into giving *Tommy* a rave review on the strength of its pinball connection.

Be that as it may, nothing takes away the sheer delight of this number, one of only two (the other was 'See Me, Feel Me') from *Tommy* to outlast the rest of the opera and remain in The Who's live set for as long as they appeared on stage.

As a single (slightly speeded up from the album version), 'Pinball' reached Number 4 in the UK charts and Number 19 in the US. Rod Stewart sang a heavily orchestrated version in Lou Reizner's all-star adaptation of *Tommy* in 1972, while Elton John sang it during a memorable set piece in Ken Russell's *Tommy* movie in 1975 (his version reached Number 7 in the UK). Curiously, in the UK, it was also covered by The New Seekers in a medley with 'See Me Feel Me', whose version reached Number 16 in 1973.

THERE'S A DOCTOR

A QUICK link into...

GO TO THE MIRROR

A NOTHER key song – Tommy discovers he can see his reflection, a leap forward in the healing process – which seamlessly juxtaposes a second refrain of 'See Me, Feel Me' with the 'Listening To You' coda into the heavier 'Mirror' riff.

TOMMY CAN YOU HEAR ME?

ROGER leads The Who in a folksy sing-along in virtual unison, accompanied only by Pete's ringing acoustic guitar and John's springy bass; lightweight but catchy.

SMASH THE MIRROR

A BRIEF, dramatic snatch highlighted by the ascending 'rise, rise rise' lyrics and the sound of breaking glass.

SENSATION

'SENSATION' was written long before *Tommy* was formulated, apparently about a girl Pete met during The Who's disastrous tour of Australia in 1968. Nevertheless, its lyrics are appropriate, as is the catchy, lightweight pop rhythm. Pete sings lead vocals.

MIRACLE CURE

A NEWSPAPER vendor offers a quick link into...

SALLY SIMPSON

'SALLY Simpson"s subject-matter may well have been one of the key elements that inspired Pete to produce *Tommy* in the first place, but it sounds as if it belongs on another album entirely. Missing are the rhythmic structures that crop up so often elsewhere, to be replaced by a rather slight melody as befits a narrative song about how Sally disobeys her parents, heads out to see Tommy perform in concert, gets caught up in a crush in front of the stage, and is permanently disfigured as a result.

The song was inspired by an incident when The Who played with The Doors at New York's Singer Bowl in August 1968. Pete apparently saw the way Jim Morrison was inciting the front row, and the dangerous situation he created.

I'M FREE

A MEMORABLE six-chord riff introduces one of the album's best songs in which Tommy throws off the shackles of his handicaps, and urges his followers – those attracted by his prowess at pinball – to follow him. Tinkly piano, a great acoustic solo, and a nice re-use of the familiar 'Pinball' intro riff.

WELCOME

T HE GENTLEST song on the album, with Roger at his most melodic, speeds up in the middle, with Roger on harmonica, and then returns to its mannered, rather dreamy aura.

TOMMY'S HOLIDAY CAMP
(Moon)

K EITH'S sole writing credit on Tommy is one minute of Pete's vocal over a fairground barrel organ extolling the virtues of the holiday camp, which Tommy has established as a base for his mission. It was Keith's idea to introduce a holiday camp into the story.

WE'RE NOT GONNA TAKE IT (SEE ME, FEEL ME)

TWO SONGS in one, the first a catchy riff based piece about rejecting fascism and the second a circular, looping prayer for unification. With its churning major chords, the finale to *Tommy* is among the most simple, yet effective pieces of music that Pete Townshend has ever written. 'See Me, Feel Me' is the most obvious hymn to Baba – or any deity – in The Who's catalogue, although there are other less obvious examples in the *Lifehouse* cycle of songs and in *Quadrophenia*. 'Listening to you...' is crystal clear homage and when it was played live it appeared for all the world as if The Who were paying a remarkable tribute to the audience they were singing to. In this respect, it couldn't fail to lift the spirits – just as all hymns are designed to do.

Bonus Tracks (Outtakes and Demos) on Deluxe Edition CD 2:

ALTHOUGH SOME TRACKS DON'T STAND UP TO REPEATED LISTENING, the bonus disc succeeds as a revelatory look at the *Tommy* creative process. Highlights have to be the studio version of 'Young Man Blues' and Pete's demos.

I WAS

A BIZARRE and brief (seventeen seconds) fragment, consisting of The Who (and friends) chanting wordlessly on high in "praise Allah" fashion. With the frustrating absence of any explanatory notes from Pete Townshend as to the origins of these out-cuts, its only possible to speculate that this might have been intended as a link piece for use in the adulatory atmosphere surrounding 'Sally Simpson' or 'Tommy's Holiday Camp'.

CHRISTMAS (OUT-TAKE 3)

AN UNUSED backing track to an alternate take of 'Christmas'. While the song itself was very much an example of how Pete constructed certain *Tommy* ideas to move the story along, this strangely riveting performance shows how Pete, John, and (especially) Keith interlocked with each other to powerful instrumental effect.

COUSIN KEVIN MODEL CHILD

THIS unreleased *Tommy* track, written by Pete and sung by Keith was ultimately rejected in favour of John's 'Cousin Kevin'. It was first released as a bonus track on the *Odds & Sods* revamped CD (1998), although it appears here in slightly remixed form.

YOUNG MAN BLUES (VERSION 1)
(Allison)

THIS 'first version' was originally released on *The House That Track Built*, a 1969 UK only sampler from The Who's label Track Records. Originally intended as a stopgap single, while The Who engrossed themselves with the Deaf, Dumb and Blind Boy, the studio cut doesn't quite cut the mustard in comparison to the highly dynamic version The Who were delivering on stage at the time (and heard to full effect on *Live At Leeds*). A slower, alternate take (version 2) was accidentally issued as a bonus track on the *Odds & Sods* CD (1998) – see entry.

TOMMY CAN YOU HEAR ME? (ALTERNATE VERSION)

RATHER than the familiar acoustic version this early take is played as an ensemble performance with an extended ending that eventually falls apart. Listen to Keith's "ooh ya ooh ya" grunt at the end, the catch-phrase of Lennie Hastings, an eccentric British jazz drummer from the time.

TRYING TO GET THROUGH

BASED around a hypnotic crunching riff that The Who had been kicking around on stage and in the studio for some time, this would appear to be an impromptu performance worked out on the studio floor under Pete's guidance, sung from the point of view of either of Tommy's parents. "Keep that going," he urges Keith as the tempo eventually shifts down a gear and the song gradually drifts off.

SALLY SIMPSON (OUT-TAKES)

A CLASSIC example of Pete and Keith as the 'Pete'n'Dud' comedy duo in the 'Oo. As engineer Damon Lyon Shaw announces the first take Pete mock announces that he's discovered his band nickname ("Bone") through the pages of English weekly music paper *Record Mirror*. This causes considerable mirth, particularly Keith with his incessant Robert Newton cackle, setting the tone for Takes 1 –5; a series of breakdowns and false starts, underlining that though the subject matter of *Tommy* was often heavy and solemn, the recording sessions were, on the whole, anything but.

MISS SIMPSON

A COMPLETED, though listless take this time, under the original working title.

WELCOME (TAKE 2)

A FAIRLY uninteresting traipse through the backing track to Take 2 of 'Welcome', which only really attracts interest when the key shifts up at 2:17 for a repeat of the "ask along that man who's wearing a carnation" sequence. This idea was later dropped.

TOMMY'S HOLIDAY CAMP (BAND'S VERSION)
(Moon)

A N EARLY rejected group performance of Keith's theme, featuring the melody line played on fairground-style organ and Moon bashing happily along behind.

WE'RE NOT GONNA TAKE IT (ALTERNATE VERSION)

T HIS early version follows Pete's original demo in that the song ends as it began with the opening riff repeating, ending on a final flourish. Of course, Pete re-thought the ending, writing the "listening to you" coda as one of the last pieces of work on *Tommy* – elevating a merely good song to something more.

DOGS (PART 2)
(Moon/Towser/Jason)

K EITH LED this powerful instrumental jam, recorded during the *Tommy* sessions, from the front, back and sides by doing what he did best: pounding his heart out on the skins. Keith, John and Pete all take solos in a frenzied, garage band style rave-up. Along with 'Cobwebs And Strange' this is the nearest thing to a Keith Moon drum solo in the entire Who catalogue.

Being released in March 1969 as the B-side of 'Pinball Wizard' (and here in a noticeably different stereo remix) would have earned its composers a tidy sum in royalties: one can only ponder how Towser and Jason, Pete and John's respective pet dogs, spent their cash!

Stereo Only Demos

IT'S A BOY

AMAZING JOURNEY

CHRISTMAS

DO YOU THINK IT'S ALRIGHT?

PINBALL WIZARD

PETE'S original stereo demos for *Tommy* have appeared on various bootlegs over the years but none have sounded as fresh and clear as Pete's remix of this humble selection (the only tracks not to appear in 5.1 sound). All five demonstrate the extraordinary ability of the part of The Who's principal composer to make wonderful recordings of his songs entirely by himself.

'Pinball Wizard' was first officially made available as part of a two track flexidisc given away with Richard Barnes' Who biography, *Maximum R&B* (1982).

Live At Leeds

Original UK issue: Track 2406 001, released May 1970;
UK CD: Polydor 825 339-2, 'remastered', 1995. Polydor 527 169-2,
Deluxe Edition Polydor 112 618-2, 2001.
US Decca DL 79175 released May 1970; CD: MCA MCAD-37000,
MFSL UDCD 755, 'remixed' CD MCA MCAD-11215 and 11230, 1995,
Deluxe Edition E+CD MCA 088 112 618-2, 2001

RECORDED ON VALENTINE'S DAY, FEBRUARY 14, 1970 AT LEEDS UNIVERSITY, *Live At Leeds* was the best live rock album of its era and remains as the paramount testament to the sheer power this little quartet could generate on stage. It was designed to spotlight the other, non-*Tommy*, side of The Who, the rough and ready 'in-yer-face' rock band that they'd always been before conceptual artistry side-tracked their principal writer. "Some people think the band's called *Tommy* and the album's called The Who," muttered Entwistle. *Live At Leeds* put a stop to that.

Its packaging was also an antidote to the grandiosity of *Tommy*: a plain buff sleeve, roughly rubber stamped with the band's name, designed to resemble a bootleg. Within could be found an envelope containing all sorts of facsimile Who ephemera (photos, date sheets, contracts, lyrics) and a record on which there was a handwritten warning that crackles heard throughout were not the fault of your record player (the remastered 1995 CD amended the note to say the crackling noises had been noise corrected!).

To watch The Who live at the tail end of the Sixties on a good night was to experience the very best that live rock could offer, anywhere in the world. This album, a few stray bits of video footage and as yet unreleased tapes, are all that remain as evidence to support the claim that The Who were the world's best when it came to live performance. On this showing the claim is unequivocally upheld.

Live At Leeds has undergone two upgrades since this book was first published. The first incorporated eight extra songs from the concert, while the second featured the entire concert spread over two CDs, the non-*Tommy* songs on CD1 with *Tommy* occupying all of CD2. While most would have preferred to have had the concert's original running order left intact, that would have required ending the first disc somewhere in the middle of *Tommy*. This approach keeps the original reason for *Leeds* in focus, with *Tommy* deliberately set aside.

Live At Leeds reached Number 3 in the UK album charts and Number 4 in the US.

The original LP and CD consisted of just six tracks:

YOUNG MAN BLUES
(Mose Allison)

MOSE ALLISON'S blues song, which the jazz pianist had first recorded in 1957 for his Prestige album *Back Country Suite*, was originally titled simply 'Blues'. The song was performed during The Who's early incarnation as The High Numbers in 1964, and was resurrected as 'Young Man Blues' in 1968, and routinely used during the *Tommy* tours of 1969/70.

At Leeds University, the song is given a whole new lease of life in The Who's violent stop-start reading, with Keith leading the assault against Roger's vocals, John contributing his usual high-speed runs and Pete slashing away on a blues riff until the solo allows him to stretch out. The version here is tighter and more assured than usual, not quite as long as they sometimes played it (thanks to some judicious editing) but hugely impressive as a showcase for The Who's wayward streams.

SUBSTITUTE

TOWNSHEND'S first comment on illusion... he always said The Who were a substitute for The Rolling Stones. This short, sharp, snappy 'Substitute' is as tight a performance as any live version around, although it lacks the punchy solo and false ending of the single.

See additional comments under *Meaty Beaty Big & Bouncy* in COMPILATIONS.

SUMMERTIME BLUES
(Eddie Cochran/Jerry Capehart)

EDDIE Cochran's bouncy, rhythmic guitar style influenced Pete enormously in The Who's early days and their version of 'Summertime Blues' was a highlight of the band's stage shows for many years. Pete's block chord slash style, coupled with John's rumbling bass riff, was ideal for this song of teenage angst, and Roger, eternally a rocker at heart, loved to sing it. John always supplied the deep bass vocal line with a wry smile. Cochran died in a car crash in the UK in 1960 and by 1968 The Who had made 'Summertime Blues' their very own, but there's no question that Eddie would have been proud that his best-known song had become a staple in the set list of a live act as great as The Who. Also released as a single in 1970.

Other Cochran songs essayed by The Who included 'C'mon Everybody' and the lesser known 'My Way' (see *Odds & Sods*).

SHAKIN' ALL OVER
(Fred Heath)

WITH THE possible exception of 'Move It', 'Dynamite' and 'It'll Be Me' – the only decent records Cliff Richard has ever released – 'Shakin' All Over' is the sole pre-Beatles UK rock'n'roll song of any serious merit, and, by far, the best. With its startling guitar riff, heavy bass line, minor key and lyrics that really do shake and rock, 'Shakin' All Over' sounds like it could have been written by one of the great American Fifties rock songwriters, such as Eddie Cochran or Leiber & Stoller.   Instead it was written by Fred Heath (a.k.a. Johnny Kidd) the leader of The Pirates, one of the first truly ballsy rock'n'roll bands in Britain. Contemporaries of The Detours (as The Who were then known), it was The Pirates, with their singer, guitar, bass and drums line-up, who convinced Roger Daltrey that he should abandon playing guitar and occupy centre stage himself. That left Pete as the sole guitarist, who took no little notice of Pirates' guitarist Mick Green whenever the two bands shared a bill.

The Who's 'Shakin' All Over' is a typical full-frontal assault, guaranteed to rouse anyone within earshot. Everyone gets a chance to shine, especially Roger who loves singing a good rocker. In concert The Who speeded up in the middle and occasionally segued into Willie Dixon's 'Spoonful' and then back again into 'Shakin' for the finale. In fact, they did this at Leeds as the unedited tapes reveal.

MY GENERATION

'MY GENERATION' went through many transformations whenever The Who played it live. Often it became a slow blues that gradually speeded up but here, on what must be one of the longest versions of the song that The Who ever performed, it starts traditionally before meandering off after the bass solo into reprised sections from *Tommy*, including a whipped-up verse of 'See Me, Feel Me', some unsecured blues and R&B hollering, and some excellent soloing by Pete who appears to play against his own echo bouncing off the back of the hall. There are many false endings and Pete often silences the band before heading off into uncharted territory, apparently finishing the song on several occasions, only to restart and accelerate again.

This version of 'My Generation' is as good an example as any of the way in which The Who could play off each other when they were in the mood. By now, barring Keith, they'd been playing together on stage for around eight years, and there's no substitute for intuition built on such experience. Listen for Keith's repeated sixth-sense count-ins, all pre-empted by a Pete line that's familiar only to him and John, and – as ever – listen to John working overtime as he zooms up and down the longest bass fretboard in rock.

For sheer exhilarating Who at their absolute live best, this track, all 14 minutes of it, takes some beating.

MAGIC BUS

WITH ITS Bo Diddley beat and room for stretching out on guitar, Pete loved to play 'Magic Bus' but John, anchored to a 'dub du-du du-du-dub, dub dub' riff on 'A', hated it. There wasn't much opportunity for Keith either, but he always looked pleased as punch to be making silly faces and tapping away on his claves while Pete and Roger swapped those preposterous lines about trading the magic bus in for 'one hundred English pounds'.

As a single, 'Magic Bus' was a minor hit in 1968. As a stage number, it became a crowd favourite if for no other reason than it was quite unlike anything else The Who ever performed. Like everything else on *Leeds* bar 'Substitute', the version here is extended well beyond its normal running time. It's also a great showcase for Pete, and Roger is no slouch on harmonica either. Sharp-eared listeners may pick out Pete's gestating riff for 'Don't Know Myself' during the closing bars.

The First Upgrade

THE 1995 CD VERSION OF *LEEDS* CONSISTED OF 14 TRACKS. (THE TWO CATALOGUE numbers for the American version represent a regular CD release and a CD in a special box set, the size of a 12" album, so that full-size reproductions of the original enclosures could be included.)

The 'remixed' or 'remastered' CD (depending on what cover blurb came with the CD) interspersed eight songs in their proper order from the concert as follows: 'Heaven And Hell', 'I Can't Explain', 'Fortune Teller', 'Tattoo', 'Young Man Blues', 'Substitute', 'Happy Jack', 'I'm A Boy', 'A Quick One, While He's Away', 'Amazing Journey'/'Sparks', 'Summertime Blues'. 'Shakin' All Over', 'My Generation', 'Magic Bus'.

An edit occurs at 1:15 into 'Magic Bus'. On the original release at this point Pete inexplicably took out 15 seconds of linking guitar and incorporated an edit of backwards guitar tape. For the remastered CD, three seconds of the proper link have been restored (you'll need the bootlegs to hear how 'Magic Bus' and 'Young Man Blues' should sound untampered with!).

The Second Upgrade
(The Deluxe Edition)

THIS **2001** VERSION INCLUDED THE ENTIRE CONCERT, BUT AS NOTED ABOVE NOT in the original order. Since all of *Tommy* is included on the second disc, 'Amazing Journey' / 'Sparks' is dropped from the first disc (see above). The net result is a release that is far beyond the intent and scope of the original LP, and frankly an unadulterated delight. The concert was one of The Who's best and easily merited a complete release.

Disc 1

HEAVEN AND HELL
(Entwistle)

ALTHOUGH recorded in the studio, but not to John or The Who's complete satisfaction, 'Heaven And Hell' was one of the best songs that John Entwistle contributed to The Who's catalogue. A harsh warning about the perils of mortal misbehaviour, it's a full-blooded rocker, rhythmically tougher than most of the material that Pete was writing at the time but still finely tuned towards The Who's particular strengths. Often used to open Who sets during the late Sixties when *Tommy* got a full airing, it allowed Pete plenty of opportunity to stretch out on the solo and the whole band could warm up for the lengthy set that lay ahead.

Originally recorded at IBC Studios, London, April 13, 1970, the studio version was released on July 10, 1970, as the 'B' side of the 'Summertime Blues' single.

See also *Rarities Volume II*.

I CAN'T EXPLAIN

THE WHO'S first single was an unashamed attempt at copying the riff style of The Kinks, and perhaps the best testament to 'Explain' is that throughout their career, The Who almost always opened their live shows with it. Live, Keith would chirp in on the high backing vocals unless sound engineer Bob Pridden discreetly switched off his mike!

See additional comments under *My Generation* LP.

FORTUNE TELLER
(Naomi/Neville)

BENNY Spellman's 1962 minor hit, also covered by The Rolling Stones and many other Sixties beat groups, 'Fortune Teller' was a staple of The Who's live act between 1968 and 1970. Opening as a medium-paced R&B lurcher, The Who slip into a higher gear halfway through, turning the song into a full-throated rocker, a fine example of 'Maximum R&B'.

The Who recorded a studio version at Advision in London on May 29, 1968, but it remained unreleased until The Who's box set, *30 Years Of Maximum R&B*, appeared in 1994.

TATTOO

SEGUED straight from 'Fortune Teller', cascading arpeggios herald 'Tattoo'. A stand-out track from their third album, *The Who Sell Out*, The Who retained their affection for 'Tattoo' long after all its other songs had been discarded. They were performing the song live right up to the mid-Seventies.

See additional comments under *The Who Sell Out* LP.

YOUNG MAN BLUES

SUBSTITUTE

ABOVE two as per original release (see above).

HAPPY JACK

THE STAR of the show here is Keith, whose remarkable drum patterns carry not only a beat that explodes on the choruses, but, in a startlingly original fashion, the melody as well. All of The Who's Sixties trademarks are present and correct: high harmonies, quirky subject matter, fat bass, and drums that suspend belief.

(See *Meaty Beaty Big & Bouncy* in COMPILATIONS)

I'M A BOY

A TIGHT, dramatic version of The Who's 1966 single with tight harmonies and a firm grasp of dynamics.

(See *Meaty Beaty Big & Bouncy* in COMPILATIONS)

A QUICK ONE, WHILE HE'S AWAY

BY 1970 The Who had been playing 'A Quick One' on stage for at least three years and there's a casual self-assurance to their playing on this version that cannot be found elsewhere, although it is rivaled by the exuberant version the group taped for *The Rolling Stones' Rock & Roll Circus* in December '68 (see LIVE ALBUMS).

SUMMERTIME BLUES

SHAKIN' ALL OVER

MY GENERATION

MAGIC BUS

ABOVE four as per the original release (see above note for 'Magic Bus').

Disc 2

THE SECOND DISC IS DEVOTED TO A LIVE RENDERING OF *TOMMY* WHICH INCLUDES the following songs: 'Overture', 'It's A Boy', '1921', 'Amazing Journey', 'Sparks', 'Eyesight To The Blind (The Hawker)', 'Christmas', 'The Acid Queen', 'Pinball Wizard', 'Do You Think It's Alright?', 'Fiddle About', 'Tommy Can You Hear Me?', 'There's A Doctor', 'Go To The Mirror', 'Smash The Mirror', 'Miracle Cure', 'Sally Simpson', 'I'm Free', 'Tommy's Holiday Camp', 'We're Not Gonna Take It'.

By the time The Who and *Tommy* reached Leeds, they could be forgiven for being well and truly sick of it. If they were, their performance doesn't reflect that. Pete Townshend commented on the show a couple of months later in *Rolling Stone* (May 14): "It just happened to be a good show, and it just happened to be like one of the greatest audiences we've ever played to in our whole career, just by chance. They were incredible and although you can't hear a lot of the kind of shouting and screaming in the background, they're civilised but they're crazy, you know, they're fantastic. And we played it in their own hall. And the sound is all right, it's a good atmosphere."

Extensive research among The Who's archives and collectors around the world reveals that the Leeds performance of *Tommy* is the very best concert version of the work extant. The version played in 1970 at the Isle Of Wight Festival and released in 1996 as *The Who Live At The Isle Of Wight* is inferior in many ways (see under live albums). It's possible that at some time in the future the top quality version played at the Amsterdam Concertgebouw Opera House on September 29, 1969, which was recorded for a radio broadcast and is now widely bootlegged, could also see official release.

Who's Next

Original UK issue: Track 2408 102, released July 1971;
UK CD: Polydor 813651-2, remixed and remastered Polydor 527760-2,
1995 Deluxe Edition Polydor 113 056-2; 2003
US: Decca 79182, released August 1971; CD: MCA MCAD 37217.
Gold Edition MCAD-37217, remixed and remastered MCA-11269, 1995,
MFSL UCDC 754, Deluxe Edition MCA 088 113 056-2, 2003

WHO'S NEXT **IS WIDELY REGARDED AS THE FINEST STUDIO ALBUM THE WHO** ever recorded and one of the best rock records ever. Certainly, it's far and away their most consistent in terms of quality songs – there isn't a duffer among them – and it introduces an important new element, the synthesizer, into the group's overall sound. More importantly, The Who were now at their creative peak, both as individual musicians and as a band: on stage they regularly performed with breathtaking panache, their confidence was at an all time high, and their status as one of the world's greatest rock bands was secured for eternity.

Who's Next started life as another of Pete's concepts, this one a movie/musical called *Lifehouse* which contained enough songs for a double LP, but the project became bogged down in its futuristic and philosophical complexities and was eventually reduced to a single LP and no movie. The concept of *Lifehouse* is long and bewildering, and the random nature of the songs on *Who's Next* gives little clue as to its story line, such as it was. In view of what *Who's Next* became, there is little point in trying to explain it here, but among its many ideals was Pete's design for The Who to somehow become one with their audience, to break down totally the barrier that exists between audience and performer. (For those interested in pursuing the story, visit Pete Townshend's website at www.eelpie.com where its creator offers a book co-written with Jeff Young, entitled *Lifehouse*, that is the unedited transcript for a radio play first broadcast on BBC Radio 3 in December 1999. Townshend also offers a recording of the play on *The Lifehouse Chronicles* and makes a credible argument that he had envisioned the internet when he was originally struggling with the *Lifehouse* concept.)

What makes *Who's Next* different from any of its predecessors is the clarity of sound afforded by producer Glyn Johns. Kit Lambert was the perfect foil for Pete to bounce ideas off and his creative influence on The Who cannot be over emphasised, but he was no technician, and as hi-fi equipment and recording studios became more and more sophisticated during the Seventies, far greater attention was being paid to the way records actually sounded. The second great leap forward on *Who's Next* was

Pete's introduction of the ARP 2600, an early synthesizer, into The Who's sound, most notably on 'Baba O'Riley' and 'Won't Get Fooled Again,' the two songs that open and close the album.

Unlike so many of his less imaginative peers Pete didn't use the instrument simply as a solo keyboard that could make funny noises, but as a rotating musical loop which underpinned the melody and added a sharp bite to the rhythm track. In this respect, he and Stevie Wonder were the first musicians of their generation to make proper creative use of this new and subsequently much abused electronic toy. In fact, Townshend's synthesizer style on *Who's Next* is the first appearance on a rock record of the electronic repetitive sequences, so predominant on modern pop and dance music.

There were other leaps forward too. Pete's song writing showed a sustained level of brilliance he would never again achieve (although he came close on *Quadrophenia*), John's bass lines were more melodic and as fluid as ever, and Keith managed to rein in his wilder antics while maintaining his usual key expressive role. However perhaps the greatest musical triumph belonged to Roger: the *Tommy* experience had improved his confidence as a vocalist and it shows, whether on the melodies of the beautiful 'Behind Blue Eyes' and 'The Song Is Over' or, at the other extreme, the torturous scream that climaxes 'Won't Get Fooled Again'.

Who's Next started out being recorded as *Lifehouse* in New York with Kit Lambert as producer, but the band weren't satisfied with the results and returned to London to re-record them at Olympic Studios in Barnes with Glyn Johns. Most of the songs recorded with Johns appeared on *Who's Next* while the leftovers appeared on singles and later, *Odds & Sods* (see below).

Who's Next became the only Who album to make Number 1 in the UK charts. It peaked at Number 4 in the US, but songs from the album are continually played on US 'Classic Rock' radio stations to this day.

There are now two upgraded CD versions of the album. The first followed the format of including a number of bonus tracks on a single disc. The Deluxe Edition dropped four of these bonus tracks but included additional tracks from the New York Record Plant sessions, some of which feature Leslie West on guitar and Al Kooper on organ and had previously appeared on bootlegs in rough mix form. The real treat is the second disc that features an almost complete show at London's Young Vic theatre when Pete was trying to bring *Lifehouse* to fruition. For some reason, younger listeners apparently found the roughness of the show a little disconcerting, judging by the comments posted on www.amazon.com.

Considering the brief period between Pete writing the songs and their live debut, the Young Vic material is staggering and every bit as worthwhile as the *Leeds* show. It captures The Who at their undisputed height as the greatest live rock band in the world. Because of this, if you're going to own a CD of *Who's Next*, the Deluxe Edition is the one.

The original release consisted of nine tracks:

BABA O'RILEY

THIRTY seconds of a spiralling loop, played on a Lowrey organ and fed through a synthesizer, opens the album with one of its most memorable tracks. 'Baba', of course, is Meher Baba, Pete's spiritual pal, and O'Riley, is Terry Riley, the electronic composer whose work *A Rainbow In Curved Air* inspired Pete's use of looping synthesizer riffs. Piano, voice, drums, bass and eventually guitar join in but it's the cut and thrust between Daltrey's leonine roar and Pete's tuneful pleading that gives the song its tension and best moments, though the free-form climax, a souped-up Irish jig featuring Dave Arbus (of the group East Of Eden) on violin and Keith playing as fast as he's ever played, is quite mesmerising.

"Teenage Wasteland", the starting point for Pete's imaginary generation in their search to find nirvana, became a timeless Who entity in Roger's hands, and the downright disgust at the way things had turned out (post-Woodstock) was never better expressed in rock.

Pete: "This was a number I wrote while I was doing these experiments with tapes on the synthesizer. Among my plans was to take a person out of the audience and feed information – height, weight, autobiographical details –

about the person into the synthesizer. The synthesizer would then select notes from the pattern of that person. It would be like translating a person into music. On this particular track I programmed details about the life of Meher Baba and that provided the backing for the number."

The synthesizer track that dominates 'Baba O'Riley' is part of a longer synthesizer piece that Pete released privately on a Meher Baba tribute LP *I Am* in 1972. Further sections featured on his *Psychoderelict* solo LP in 1993.

BARGAIN

MOST SONGS addressed to 'you' are sentimental love songs but the you Pete addresses in 'Bargain' is his avatar, Meher Baba. 'Bargain', which stands alongside any of the best tracks on *Who's Next*, is about the search for personal identity amid a sea of conformity, with lyrics such as "I know I'm worth nothing without you" giving the Baba slant away, especially when sung by Pete in a keening counterpoint to Roger's harsher lines.

Although there's a low-key synthesizer track in the background, 'Bargain' shows off The Who's ensemble playing at its very best. Block chords abound, there's a terrific guitar solo, bass lines pop and crackle and Keith's drumming gives the song a rhythmic foundation that lifts The Who clean out of your speaker cabinets. A terrific live version of 'Bargain' can be found on *Who's Missing* (see below).

LOVE AIN'T FOR KEEPING

SERIOUSLY upfront acoustic guitars feature strongly throughout one of the slighter (and shortest) songs on *Who's Next*, but the bouncy tempo, relatively simple compared with the album's other songs, and understated synthesizer hold this together well, as Roger sings about the difficulty of sustaining relationships in the modern world. This track is sequenced to run almost directly into...

MY WIFE
(Entwistle)

JOHN'S SONG of marital discontent gets many fans' vote for the best he ever wrote for The Who and it provided the group with a terrific stage rocker, complete with the kind of block chords that Pete loved to play while spinning his arm windmill-style. Although this version is no slouch, John was dissatisfied with the sound and re-recorded it himself on his third solo album, *Rigor Mortis Sets In* (1973). On live versions, Pete would stretch out during the song's solo and end, duelling with John to mesmerising effect. 'My Wife' is possibly the most 'Who-like' song John ever wrote, certainly the closest to Pete's writing style, and the lyrics, about his first wife, are generally hilarious.

THE SONG IS OVER

AMONG the most gorgeous ballads Pete has ever written, 'The Song Is Over' again highlights the contrasting vocals of Roger and Pete, as well as some inspired synthesizer work, tasteful piano playing by Nicky Hopkins, and a sumptuous production. Because of its complexity, it was never played live. Doubtless intended as the climax to *Lifehouse*, it features as a coda the motif from 'Pure And Easy' (see *Odds & Sods* below), another key *Lifehouse* song that was inexplicably left off the album. The closing passages are enhanced by an almost subliminal top-of-the-scale synthesizer harmonic line that traces the melody with a marvellous undulating counterpoint.

It is only by listening to this song, in conjunction with others like 'Pure And Easy', 'Baba O'Riley', 'Bargain', 'Time Is Passing' (which The Who never released) and 'Behind Blue Eyes' that the real potential of *Lifehouse*, at least from a purely musical point of view, can be truly appreciated. A rock opera, or at least a song cycle, based around material as strong as this would surely have been the rock masterpiece to end all rock masterpieces. When it failed to materialise in the way he envisaged, Pete's disillusionment led to his first nervous breakdown and almost broke up The Who.

GETTING IN TUNE

USING THE time honoured tradition of tuning up before a show as an allegory for creating harmony between disparate societies, 'Getting In Tune' is another fearless rocker, perhaps not quite so breathtaking as others from the album, but certainly no slouch. Like 'The Song Is Over', this is a showcase for Roger at his absolute best.

GOING MOBILE

WITH ITS rolling, appropriately 'mobile' rhythm and absence of harsh chords, 'Going Mobile' lacks the grandeur of many of the other tracks on *Who's Next*, but it's a witty and worthy contender nevertheless, a 'travelogue' sung by Pete about the joys of driving around gypsy-style in his newly acquired holiday home. Lines about 'hippy gypsies' seem particularly apt in the modern era of New Age travellers.

Apart from its tricky little acoustic rhythm signature, it's also notable for the guitar solo in which Pete wired his electric through a device similar to a wah-wah called an 'envelope follower', with the result that it sounds like he's playing underwater.

BEHIND BLUE EYES

OPENING with one of the prettiest melodies Pete has ever written, 'Behind Blue Eyes' rightly became a Who classic almost immediately. Crystal clear acoustic guitar, Roger at his melodic best and a fluid bass line take the first verse, velvet three-part harmonies join in for the second, then, finally, in lurches Keith to give 'Behind Blue Eyes' its third and final dimension.

The faster central passage, a plea to the creator for confidence and succour, contains the most moving lyrics on the whole album, before the song reverts back to its gentle opening lines at the close. The choir-like closing vocal harmony, drenched in reverb, is deliberately – and brilliantly – sequenced to contrast sharply with the shrill electronic synthesizer riff that heralds 'Won't Get Fooled Again'.

WON'T GET FOOLED AGAIN

IF THERE IS a key song on *Who's Next*, it is this lengthy call to arms that became the traditional show closer at Who concerts from this point onwards. Based on a clattering synthesizer riff that locks the group into a tight, rhythmic performance, 'Won't Get Fooled Again' is classic mid-period Who at their very best, Pete's block chords firmly in place, John swooping up and down his bass, Roger singing his heart out and Keith an almighty presence, albeit slightly more disciplined than usual in view of the song's inflexible structure.

With lyrics that address the futility of revolution when the conqueror is likely to become as corrupt as the conquered, the song inspired many a clenched fist, especially when Roger came careering in at the end of the lengthy instrumental passage, declaiming the 'bosses' and inciting the kind of scenes that left the Bastille in ruins. His scream before the final verse is one of the most volatile vocal eruptions ever recorded.

Pete: "It's really a bit of a weird song. The first verse sounds like a revolution song and the second like somebody getting tired of it. It's an angry anti-establishment song. It's anti people who are negative. A song against the revolution because the revolution is only a revolution and a revolution is not going to change anything at all in the long run, and a lot of people are going to get hurt."

Edited down from its original eight minutes and thirty seconds, 'Won't Get Fooled Again' as a single reached Number 9 in the UK charts and 10 in the US.

Remixed and Remastered CD

THIS VERSION KEPT THE SINGLE DISC FORMAT, ADDING THE FOLLOWING bonus tracks:

PURE AND EASY

THIS IS THE original version of 'Pure And Easy' recorded at the Record Plant, New York, on March 17-18, 1971. A later version was recorded at Olympic Studios, London, but not released until the *Odds & Sods* LP in 1974 (although, confusingly, John Entwistle recollected the recording stemmed from the preparatory sessions made at Mick Jagger's mansion, Stargroves on the Rolling Stones Mobile).

A key song from *Lifehouse*, 'Pure And Easy' is a beautiful Townshend composition that should have appeared on *Who's Next* but was left off, probably because The Who weren't 100% satisfied with the ver-sions they'd recorded during the *Lifehouse/Who's Next* sessions. It is hard to find anything wrong with the version included here.

'Pure And Easy' is Pete's re-write on the myth of the 'Lost Chord', a deeply felt song about the ultimate musical note, the loss of which symbolises mankind's decaying relationship with the universe. It is a song of yearning, almost a tearful lament, albeit fashioned over Who-style torrents. The guitar solo builds to a tremendous climax, rather like Jimmy Page's memorable solo in 'Stairway To Heaven'.

Pete thought very highly of 'Pure And Easy' when he wrote it – so much so that its chorus forms a coda to 'The Song Is Over' on *Who's Next*, and he included it in demo form on his first solo album *Who Came First*.

In the accompanying notes he wrote for *Odds And Sods*, the album on which this song first appeared in 1974, Pete wrote: "This you might know from my solo album. This is the group's version. Not all of the group's versions of my songs are as faithful to the original demo as this one, but as usual The 'Oo make their terrible mark. Another track from the aborted *Lifehouse* story. It's strange, really, that this never appeared on *Who's Next*, because in the context of stuff like 'Song Is Over', 'Getting In Tune' and 'Baba O'Riley' it explains more about the general concept behind the Lifehouse idea than any amount of rap. Not released because we wanted a single album at the time."

It's remarkable to think that at this stage in his evolution as a songwriter (1971) Pete Townshend was able to discard material as strong as this.

The Who performed 'Pure And Easy' on stage briefly during 1971, on stage at the Young Vic and occasionally thereafter.

BABY DON'T YOU DO IT
(Holland/Dozier/Holland)

A STAGE favourite of The Who's from the 1964-66 era, this Marvin Gaye Motown classic was perhaps an unusual choice for revival for *Lifehouse*. Played at the Young Vic and in the concert act for the remainder of 1971, this version was recorded at the Record Plant, New York on March 16, 1971. Leslie West guested on lead guitar.

NAKED EYE

T HIS WAS recorded live at The Young Vic on April 26, 1971, and first released as part of the 1994 *30 Years of Maximum R&B* box set. A studio version, recorded at Pete's Eel Pie Studio in 1970 appeared on the *Odds & Sods* LP in 1974.

A superb stage song, 'Naked Eye' was developed on stage as part of the improvisation during extended versions of 'My Generation' (see *Live At Leeds*) and, once fully formed, played at virtually every Who concert in the early Seventies. It took on enormous power as Pete and Roger shared verses that contained some of Pete's most powerful lyrical imagery ever.

Between oblique references to drugs and guns is a deep sense of frustration and failure, of not knowing where next to run to, yet at the same time realising that to stand still is suicidal, matters uppermost in Pete's mind as he sought to justify his continued role in The Who and The Who's continued existence. Meanwhile the band strains at the leash, while a strange nagging riff holds the song together. This is the riff that made its first appearance at concerts during 1969 when the band were jamming at the climax to their shows, and only later did Pete add lyrics to harness it into 'Naked Eye'.

Like 'Pure And Easy', 'Naked Eye' is an essential Who song, far more important than many found elsewhere in the catalogue.

WATER

ALSO RECORDED at the same Young Vic show as above.

An overlong, rather heavy-handed rocker, 'Water' is another *Lifehouse* reject, this one mixing a rather lascivious hook line ('water' rhymes with 'daughter' throughout) into a song in which 'water' becomes an allegory for quenching spiritual thirst. Considering the role it played on stage, it seemed destined for inclusion on whatever album that would follow *Tommy*. Eventually Pete came up with several far better songs, and despite several stage comments at various shows and concerts during 1970/71 introducing it as a possible Who single, 'Water' was consigned to the scrap heap, only to resurface as the UK B-side of '5.15' in October 1973.

TOO MUCH OF ANYTHING

ANOTHER *Lifehouse* outtake, produced by The Who, and associate producer Glyn Johns, at Olympic Studios, London, April 12, 1971. It was first released in 1974, with Roger's re-recorded vocal, on *Odds & Sods*.

'Too Much Of Anything' is a rather pedestrian rock ballad, with Nicky Hopkins on piano, that deals with greed and its consequences, but the song meanders along indifferently without the punch of other *Lifehouse* tracks. The Who occasionally played it on stage in 1971 but soon dropped it.

I DON'T EVEN KNOW MYSELF

THIS IS A 1970 Eel Pie recording that was part of a planned EP project. Instead, it appeared as the B-side to the 'Won't Get Fooled Again' single in June 1971, credited as 'Don't Know Myself'. A *Lifehouse* reject which wasn't quite up to the standard of the other songs Pete was writing in 1970, 'I Don't Know Even Know Myself' blends a fierce verse and chorus with a strange, country and western style middle eight which features Keith tapping a wooden block. Often played live in 1970/71, but dropped when *Who's Next* provided the band with better stage material.

BEHIND BLUE EYES

THIS original version of 'Behind Blue Eyes' was recorded at the Record Plant, New York, on March 17-18, 1971, and features Al Kooper on organ.

Deluxe Edition

THE FIRST CD CONTAINS THE NINE TRACKS OFF THE ORIGINAL ALBUM AND THE following bonus tracks from the Record Plant Sessions, New York, March 1971.

BABY DON'T YOU DO IT
(Holland/Dozier/Holland)

WHILE THE remixed and remastered CD featured a 5:13 edit with Keith's barely audible comment, "put away your girlie magazines" at the start, the Deluxe Edition featured a new 8:20 remix of the complete version, with Roger's barked "a bit of quiet please" command before starting and an outbreak of laughter when the track finally winds down.

GETTING IN TUNE

AN ALTERNATIVE version from the Record Plant sessions, recorded March 18, 1971. Previously unreleased.

PURE AND EASY

THIS IS THE same take as on the remixed and remastered CD, except it has been freshly remixed and has a full ending instead of fading at 4:19.

LOVE AIN'T FOR KEEPING

ORIGINALLY produced by Kit Lambert, this version of 'Love Ain't For Keeping' was recorded on March 17, 1971. It features a live vocal from Pete, and Leslie West on second guitar. Previously available on the revamped *Odds & Sods* CD in 1998, the *Who's Next* version was recorded with Glyn Johns at Olympic Studios in London two months later.

BEHIND BLUE EYES

THIS IS THE same track as on the remixed and remastered CD.

WON'T GET FOOLED AGAIN

THIS IS AN early version of the song from the Record Plant sessions, recorded on March 16, 1971, featuring a different synthesizer pattern than the released version, with the famous lyric "Meet the new boss, same as the old boss", occurring *before* the final synthesizer break and drum pattern, and lacking Roger's memorable scream.

Pete: "No tape was used. What

we did was play an organ through a VCS3 live with the session. So we had to keep in time with the square wave, but the shape was moveable. It was an experiment initiated by Roger and was fairly successful."

Deluxe Edition Disc 2

PETE HAD ANTICIPATED USING LIVE MATERIAL FROM A NUMBER OF SMALL concerts before a specially invited audience to help develop the *Lifehouse* project. The Young Vic Theatre, a venue close to Waterloo Station with a reputation for the *avant garde*, was booked each Monday and the Rolling Stones Mobile was hired for what appears to have been the final *Lifehouse* show on April 26, 1971 (where the tracks on the second disc emanate from).

Also recorded at this show but left off because of space restrictions were: 'Baby Don't You Do It', 'Pinball Wizard', 'See Me, Feel Me', and 'Boney Maronie' (see *30 Years Of Maximum R&B*).

By all accounts, the *Lifehouse* experiment was physically and mentally frustrating for Pete, and the tapes were quietly shelved as he failed to bring the concept into a format his fellow band members and audience could understand.

LOVE AIN'T FOR KEEPING

A S INFORMAL an introduction a Who concert could ever produce, this was the electric version of 'Love Ain't For Keeping' The Who used to open their UK and US concerts over the summer of 1971. Considering that this (and the majority of the Young Vic material) were working versions of what were then unreleased songs, The Who clearly show they were masters of their craft, if somewhat mystified at what Pete was trying to produce. Entwistle and Moon's interlocking playing is particularly noteworthy.

PURE AND EASY

A VERY good version with Pete's guitar solo not quite as developed as the recorded take, but with John's trebly bass figures well to the fore. The additional verse from Pete's demo (lopped off for the recorded version) is still intact. The transition to "There once was a note, Listen!" is well handled in the latter part of the performance with more fine Townshend soloing.

YOUNG MAN BLUES
(Allison)

THE BAND begin aggressively enough, if not with quite the flair as at *Live At Leeds*, but Pete's guitar goes dead at 1:40 (one can only imagine the stage demonstration in anger management that Pete is *not* exercising!). While his guitar gets seen to, Entwistle and Moon carry on a breathless display of interplaying for 30 seconds without the slightest need for a lead guitarist or vocalist. Pete kicks back in and vents his frustration in a great guitar run until he peels off into a very beautiful blues orientated solo.

TIME IS PASSING

THIS VERSION highlights the great mix on the Deluxe Edition's second disc, best heard in the contrast between Pete's and Roger's vocals. 'Time Is Passing' was first widely heard on Townshend's solo album *Who Came First*, which was released in September 1972. Originally recorded during the Olympic *Who's Next* sessions, a remastered Who studio version from a damaged master tape was released on the upgraded edition of *Odds & Sods* in 1998.

BEHIND BLUE EYES

INTRODUCED as "probably a single", this live version is unusual in that

Keith is still seated behind his drums during the opening verses (playing cymbal flourishes) when traditionally he was banished from the stage. He comes in on the beat with impeccable timing.

I DON'T EVEN KNOW MYSELF

PETE FIRST rebukes a fan that dared to stand up and 'idiot dance' during the previous song. Pete explains that he normally wouldn't care, but it is distracting as The Who are playing "a whole new show". An excellent version as is to be expected for a song The Who had played live for the past year.

TOO MUCH OF ANYTHING

PETE INTRODUCES the song by smoking a cigar to celebrate the recent birth of his second daughter, Aminta. When a heckler pipes up, Pete retorts with "because I've had more fucks than you've had mate... Many more... When you catch up, come round". Although Roger starts off in a key that is comfortable for his range, as the song progresses, he strains to hit the high notes. A good attempt, nevertheless and fascinating to see what worked well on stage for the band while developing what came to be known as *Who's Next*.

GETTING IN TUNE

THIS SOUNDS faster than the album version, and lasts for over six and a half minutes. John's bass line doesn't sound fully developed yet, and at 4:10, the bass and guitar cut out as Roger, John and Pete repeatedly sing the pay-off line "Getting in tune to the straight and narrow".

BARGAIN

PETE apologises that the new songs are "sounding a wee bit lame, but they'll come together". This version is played a little slower – the tempo throws Moon into some confusion – but is noteworthy primarily for the lack of synthesizer that dominates the album version. The song was refined and went on to be one of the exhilarating highlights of the Who's 1971/72 shows (check out the live version on *Who's Missing* and *30 Years Of Maximum R&B*) for confirmation, so why it wasn't retained in the act remains a mystery.

WATER

IN A LIVE context, The Who often dragged this slight song out to an inordinate length – no exception here at 8:19 (this Young Vic version first appeared in edited form on *30 Years Of Maximum R&B* and the remastered *Who's Next* [1995]).

While it's debatable whether it merited such an approach, it was a cornerstone of Who shows throughout 1970/71. A studio version eventually appeared on the B-side of '5.15' in October 1973.

MY GENERATION

"NOT TRYING to cause a *b-b-bloody* big sensation," as Rogers sings. This is a straightforward treatment of the classic and is terminated by Pete sliding his pick up the strings to herald...

ROAD RUNNER
(Ellas McDaniel)

ORIGINALLY written and recorded by blues master Bo Diddley (a.k.a. Ellas McDaniel) in 1959, the song has subsequently been covered by many artists, including Jr. Walker & The All-Stars' hit instrumental version in 1966. During the British R&B boom of the early to mid-Sixties many groups covered Bo's classic including The Rolling Stones, The Animals, The Pretty Things, The Zombies, and The Who. (In fact, it was this very song that the group played during Keith Moon's drum-damaging audition at the Oldfield Hotel, Greenford, in April 1964.) During tours in the Seventies The Who often lurched into this medium paced rocker during lengthy jams within the 'My Generation' framework.

Pete: "It was an afterthought to

play this, probably not a good idea. It was a chaotic evening and I think that during this song some young boys started to fiddle around with some older women who were present, one of whom was Roger's ex, Cleo. We lost concentration as there were no bouncers."

NAKED EYE

SHARP-EARED Who aficionados can pinpoint that this song (and certainly the middle break) had its genesis in parts of Pete's guitar work played during the 'My Generation' finale of The Who's set at Woodstock.

A long-standing concert favourite, this version is slightly marred by Roger forgetting the lyrics during the final verse. A studio version was recorded at Eel Pie Sound in 1970 (completed at Olympic on June 7, 1971) and released in 1974 on *Odds & Sods*.

WON'T GET FOOLED AGAIN

THE WHO'S second epic single (after 'I Can See For Miles') was pretty well worked out at this stage (possibly because it had already been recorded). There are some interesting guitar runs played over the synthesizer, with Roger's definitive rock and roll scream at the conclusion, but the recorded version has a little extra drive and aggression.

Quadrophenia

Original UK issue: Track 2657 013, released November 1973;
CD: Polydor 831 072-2, remixed and remastered Polydor 531 971-2, 1996.
US: MCA2 10004, released October 1973; CD: MCA MCAD 2-6895,
remastered gold disc MFSL UDCD 2-550, remixed and remastered
MCA MCAD2-11463, 1996.

IF *TOMMY* WAS A CAREER TURN IN THE WHO'S HISTORY, REPRESENTING A changeover from a mod or pop singles band into an album orientated rock band, *Quadrophenia* represented an equally significant change. The Who had now moved from being a rock group into becoming Pete's foil. *Lifehouse* proved that when no band member stepped in to suggest a way forward, the project fell apart. Instead, the other three were prepared to wait for Pete's next big idea. In hindsight, *Quadrophenia* was almost completely Pete's baby, indicated by the lack of any room for a contribution from John or the use of any other outside sources.

The general rock audience and most Who fans were probably unaware of these developments because so little (at the time) was known about the collapse of *Lifehouse*, out of which, had come one of rock's greatest albums. *Quadrophenia* can now be seen as leading directly to *The Who By Numbers*, generally accepted as a Townshend solo effort featuring The Who. All of which leads to the question: Just what is *Quadrophenia* about?

The Who were often accused of being obsessed with their own history, and while 'obsessed' might be too strong a word, there is no doubt that their experiences as a band – and a band's experiences of life – offered Pete Townshend a rich seam of subject matter to chronicle in his songs. No better example can be found in The Who's catalogue than *Quadrophenia* which brought together several essential elements of Townshend's style: the song cycle, the synthesizers he'd pioneered on *Who's Next*, adolescent frustration, the search for spiritual contentment and an effort to try and reconcile his own past, especially the Mod experience which he'd observed in 1964/65 and which was so closely wrapped up in The Who's story. In doing so Townshend produced his most mature masterpiece, probably the most underrated Who album of all, and one which continues to fascinate new converts 30 odd years after its initial release.

Unfortunately, while the timing for the release of *Tommy* was prescient, *Quadrophenia* arrived at a time when lengthy rock works were beginning to lose their charm. In 1973 rock fans seemed less inclined to sit through and assimilate so much material at one stretch as they were in 1969. By 1976, three minute explosions – courtesy of the punk vanguard –

would be *au courrant* and works like *Quadrophenia* roundly vilified; not that The Who hadn't blazed a trail with three minute explosions of their own, of course; but that was conveniently forgotten by their critics.

There were also problems playing *Quadrophenia* live. At their best The Who were a free-flowing, high energy machine, capable of improvising at will and flying off at remarkable tangents, usually on the spur of the moment at Pete's whim. The backing tapes of synthesizer music, which were needed to present a substantial chunk of *Quadrophenia* authentically on stage, dictated a different approach, a more rigid style, and allowed little room for The Who to play together in the manner in which they excelled. When the tapes didn't gel with The Who, or The Who didn't gel with the tapes, or – even worse – when the tapes came in at the wrong time and threw everyone off balance, *Quadrophenia* came crashing down, reducing Pete to a spluttering rage. The other three, eager to please but concerned that Pete occasionally aimed too high, grew equally frustrated. So, too, did the fans. Eventually, rather like *Tommy*, *Quadrophenia* was edited down, and only four songs: '5.15', 'Drowned', 'The Punk And The Godfather' and 'Love Reign O'er Me' survived as live pieces, though special mention must be made of 'Bell Boy', Keith's vocal spotlight which would remain a crowd favourite while he was around to perform it.

One interesting proposition is whether The Who gave *Quadrophenia* sufficient time to work out its presentation problems. What could have happened if the band had added a keyboard player in 1973 for its live appearances? At the time, The Who, alone of major rock groups, found it impossible to contemplate supplementing the band with back up or other studio musicians on stage. The successful 1996/97 *Quadrophenia* tour, with its 'cast of thousands' indicates the success and public acceptance that might have been achieved earlier.

Quadrophenia is the story of the journey of a Mod by the name of Jimmy, whose restlessness, frustration, and ultimate disillusionment drive him almost to suicide. It takes in many Mod concerns – clothes, style, Brighton trips, pills and even a Who concert – and ends on a note of triumph when Jimmy somehow manages to free himself from the shackles of the cult. Each member of The Who has his own musical theme in *Quadrophenia* and each represents one facet of Jimmy's 'quadraphonic' personality, although this aspect of *Quadrophenia* is never fully explored. Of course, none of The Who were true Mods. Roger and John were rockers at heart, Keith was into surf music and wanted to be a Beach Boy, and Pete was an art student with an inquisitive mind who latched on to Mods at the suggestion of early manager Pete Meaden as a way to further the band's career. But this didn't stop Pete from observing the Mods' way of life, their rituals and dances, and sympathising with their attitudes. *Quadrophenia* was his debt to the cult of Mod and, in many ways, the album and film have become lasting Mod icons, the film especially a historical record of the Mod heritage.

Quadrophenia was immaculately packaged in a handsome black and white gatefold sleeve, complete with extensive liner notes telling Jimmy's story and a 22-page book of evocative black and white photographs illustrating his personal odyssey. Released to coincide with The Who's first UK & US tours for two years, it reached Number 2 in both countries' album charts.

As far as technical upgrades went, MFSL remastered a gold disc in the US but it had a disappointing overall sound (Roger and John often complained about their parts in the original mix of *Quadrophenia*). The remixed and remastered CDs have their proponents, but frankly don't sound as good as the original Japanese vinyl release.

Finally, for those who consider *Quadrophenia* just a little too far ahead of its time, think about the album's title. In the early Seventies, Quadraphonic sound was touted as the next big technical development in the music industry and Pete was clearly aware of it as an influence on his project. In 1973, the process proved too complicated and unworkable. At the time of writing, a planned upgrade that will involve a SACD hybrid version of *Quadrophenia*, hopefully with the addition of out-takes, playable in 5.1 surround (quad by any other name), may finally present Pete's troubled *meisterwerk* as he wanted us to hear it in the first place.

I AM THE SEA

OPENING with the sound of the ocean, faint echoes of the four principal *Quadrophenia* themes are heard before The Who come crashing in. The sea and storm effects are captured perfectly and, on a good stereo system, sound wonderfully realistic, better than any special effects recording. A dramatic starting link into...

blame on those whom he feels have let him down. Unadulterated rock, lifting and descending with asymmetric drum patterns and sharp guitar chords, plus the brass that features heavily throughout *Quadrophenia*. Towards the end the guitar, which is never obtrusive, cuts out completely to allow Moon and Entwistle to carry the rhythm as only they can. The latter's impromptu patterns throughout the song are truly awe inspiring and a fitting tribute to the late bassist's impeccable musicianship.

THE REAL ME

IN WHICH Roger, as Jimmy, ponders over his own identity, casting

QUADROPHENIA

AN INSTRUMENTAL piece that introduces the various themes, much as the 'Overture' did for *Tommy*. The arrangements are surprisingly sophisticated, and the poignant 'Love Reign O'er Me' section is as powerful and moving as anything on the record.

CUT MY HAIR

ONE OF the less memorable songs on the album in which Jimmy sings of his home life and the hopelessness of always trying to stay ahead of fashion. It closes with a news item about Mods and Rockers fighting on Brighton seafront read in the BBC's most formal manner by announcer John Curle.

THE PUNK AND THE GODFATHER

ARGUABLY the best track on the album, 'The Punk And The Godfather' sees Jimmy come face to face with The Who – with Pete as the Godfather – and question his allegiance. Opening with a magnificent double tracked guitar chord riff and with echoes of 'My Generation' and crowd noise, the uptempo passage fades away for one of the most evocative, autobiographical asides ("I've lived your future out, by pounding stages like a clown") Pete

has ever written, and which he sings in complete contrast to Roger's angry attack.

I'M ONE

OPENS AS a gentle, folksy ballad with finger picked guitar before the band join to bring the song into its own; about Jimmy's determination to retain his own identity regardless of what the crowd may think. With less synthesizer – and consequently less overdubs – than most of the other tracks on *Quadrophenia*, 'I'm One' has a distinct live feel to it.

THE DIRTY JOBS

IN COMPLETE contrast to the previous song, there is almost no guitar on this mid-paced track but plenty of synthesizer loops support Roger as he sings about class conflict in the workplace from the point of view of the junior at the bottom of the heap.

HELPLESS DANCER (ROGER'S THEME)

A DRAMATIC but lean Gilbert & Sullivan-style operatic aria featuring a double tracked Roger over staccato piano chords, acoustic guitar and little else. Under-arranged, short, and decidedly experimental in tone, this is the least Who-like piece on the album which is intended to reflect Jimmy's increasing political awareness, but as has been pointed out elsewhere, Mods took no interest in politics whatsoever so its sensibility is quite out of character. Not that this sort of logical argument ever really bothered Pete when it came to creating a song cycle...

IS IT IN MY HEAD?

OPENING with a snatch of 'The Kids Are Alright', this was one of the earliest songs Pete wrote for *Quadrophenia*, a medium paced ballad which speeds up on the chorus but which hasn't as strong a melody as most of the tracks on the album.

I'VE HAD ENOUGH

SOMEWHAT over-reaching itself, this song opens as a driving rocker, then jerks into a different passage before a final section in which Roger sings along country-style accompanied only by Pete on banjo. There are several songs on *Quadrophenia* that, like this, attempt to scale epic heights, including 'The Punk And The Godfather', 'Bell Boy' and 'Doctor Jimmy', but this one doesn't quite measure up because the sections don't mesh together quite so well.

5.15

THE best-known song on *Quadrophenia* and a minor hit single, '5.15' relates Jimmy's extra-sensual experiences on the train from London to Brighton sandwiched between two city gents. A memorable riff, emphasised by a horn section, it was probably too raw to be a serious chart contender, but listen out for Keith imitating the sound of train wheels decelerating, an effect he also repeated when The Who performed '5.15' live, which they often did.

SEA AND SAND

ANOTHER rather disjointed song with several different sections and tempo changes that all boil down to Jimmy deciding to sleep on the beach. There's a confusing false ending and during the final fade-out Roger echoes the "I'm the face if you want it" line from 'I'm The Face', the Mod anthem recorded by The Who in 1964 when they were known as The High Numbers.

DROWNED

A TOUGH rocker, based on Joe Cocker's 'Hitchcock Railway' (Cocker's pianist Chris Stainton plays on this track, along with '5.15' and 'The Dirty Jobs') which The Who loved to play on stage for its relative simplicity compared with certain other Quadrophenia tracks. On occasion Pete pushed the song to its ultimate limit, leaving the rest of the band shattered at the conclusion. Ultimately the overall feel of the song seems incompatible with the rest of the album.

Pete: "This song should actually stand alone... (when we were recording) it rained so hard that the walls were flowing with sheets of water. Chris Stainton played piano in a booth and when the take was finished he opened the door and about 500 gallons gushed out!"

BELL BOY (KEITH'S THEME)

A RARE Keith Moon lead vocal, shared at times with Roger, but unquestionably his best effort in The Who's catalogue. Somehow Keith manages to pitch things exactly right here, blending his usual comic persona with a wistful, nostalgic glance back to the Mod experience and how it died after the glories of Brighton beach. Of course in his heart of hearts, Keith was nothing more than an old-fashioned showman who'd do anything to raise a cheer. 'Bellboy' was among his finest cheers.

DOCTOR JIMMY (JOHN'S THEME)

A STEAMROLLER of a song and certainly the *magnum opus* on the album, although its relative complexity – it was really two songs in

one – meant that The Who never really mastered a lasting stage version.

John Atkins (*Generations* magazine): "... a towering, massive song that threatens to bludgeon all in its path with its verse and stature. Cast in the huge, grandiose style that only The Who could pull off without sounding pretentious and unwieldy... thrilling chord changes, dramatic verses and a sweeping synthesizer score. The chorus is instantly catchy but has longevity of appeal and there's enough change and variety in the arrangement to justify the length (7.59) of the song. Like on 'Bell Boy', the confidence and vigour of The Who burns through this ambitious song and, significantly, they never attempted anything quite like it again."

Pete: "All the songs from *Quadrophenia* are meant to fit together, or at least all reflect the personality of one person – as a result they are all structured similarly. But 'Dr Jimmy' is the archetype, more so in fact than *Quadrophenia* itself."

THE ROCK

T HIS IS A lengthy instrumental piece in which the four main themes in *Quadrophenia* are reprised in a different arrangement from the earlier 'Quadrophenia' track.

LOVE REIGN O'ER ME
(PETE'S THEME)

FOUR resounding notes, descending into the abyss that is both a stormy sea and Jimmy's confusion, herald the best known theme from *Quadrophenia* and a song The Who continued to perform long into the future. 'Love Reign O'er Me' reaches for greater heights than simply the climax to Jimmy's tale, and – with love as an allegory for Him – becomes a prayer to the heavens seeking absolution and contentment. Epic in scale, epic in performance and a shattering climax to a richly rewarding listening experience.

A piano based version was used as the US single, which so far has not appeared on CD.

Odds & Sods

Original UK issue: Track 2406 116, released October 1974;
UK CD: Polydor 517 946-2, remixed & remastered Polydor 539 791-2,
1998. US: MCA 2126, released October 1974; CD: MCA MCAD-1659,
remixed & remastered MCA MCAD-11718, 1998.

ODDS & SODS WAS THE WHO'S ATTEMPT AT CLEARING THE DECKS. OVER THE years they'd recorded many songs that were never released, though some of them – notably 'Naked Eye' and 'Pure And Easy' – had been played live and were well known to fans. With time on his hands while his band mates were tied up acting or working on the production of the *Tommy* movie, John Entwistle reviewed tapes stored in Track Records archives and came up with a quite remarkable collection of songs that The Who had deemed unworthy of release, either because they simply didn't fit into the mood of whatever The Who were working on at the time or, in the case of material recorded for *Lifehouse/Who's Next*, there was simply a surfeit of songs.

In some cases, perhaps The Who thought that they might one day record a better version, but whatever the motives, it says much for the band that songs of this standard (which many acts would have killed for) were simply shelved.

Odds & Sods reached Number 10 in UK and Number 15 in US. The best review of the tracks on the original release is easily Pete's liner notes included as part of the original packaging, which took the form of a track-by-track explanation. There was a longer version published in *New Musical Express* on September 21, 1974. Pete's thoughts as to what this album was all about are worth repeating, "While Roger Daltrey was groping round the *Tommy* film set playing (rather masterfully) the part of the deaf dumb and blind kid, while Keith Moon was dressed in a dirty raincoat drinking Guinness with a raw egg and flashing at passers-by, while my fairly good self was ensconced (as usual) in its studio fast asleep but very convincingly pretending to work, John Entwistle, with a little help from his friends, was rooting about in the mountain of unmarked tape boxes at Track Records. He came up with this remarkable collection of unreleased oddities, impulsively labelled *Odds & Sods* by Roger. I'm going to tell you why they were never released in the first place (and what a load of rubbish it is). Joking aside it's all perfection! Are THE WHO (pause for reverent head-bowing and hand on collar bone etc.) capable of anything less?"

For a throwaway release, however, the packaging, designed by Roger's cousin, Graham Hughes, was strictly first-class. It included a double sleeve, with a cut out cover into which slipped a rather ordinary poster. There was a lyric sheet also featuring Pete's liner notes. In what was an innovative move at the time, suggested by Track's Mike Shaw, the titles of the songs were written in braille on the UK rear sleeve.

The Original Release

THE ORIGINAL ALBUM INCLUDED 11 TRACKS, SOME REMIXED OR REMASTERED versions of which appeared as bonus tracks on other CD upgrades. This almost led to *Odds & Sods* being overlooked for its own upgrade. Much of the recording information given in the liner notes is incorrect.

The correct or approximate dates are given below.

POSTCARD
(Entwistle)

PRODUCED by The Who at Pete's own Eel Pie Sound sometime during the spring of 1970. Opening with a stabbing brass riff and the well used lie, "We're having a lovely time, wish you were here", this is John's tongue-in-cheek road song which details the sights and sounds of the countries visited by The Who on recent tours, set to an up-tempo rock rhythm. Originally intended for an EP that never happened.

NOW I'M A FARMER

PRODUCED by Pete Townshend at Eel Pie during spring 1970. Recorded for the same EP as 'Postcard', this is Pete's wistful ode to the joys of an outdoor life digging in the fields. "This track is from the period when The Who went slightly mad," he wrote in the accompanying liner notes. "We put out several records called 'Dogs'..." Only Roger, at home on his farm on the Kent/Sussex border, was likely to have identified with the outdoor life, though Pete shows a natural bent towards horticulture matters during his spoken fade-out.

PUT THE MONEY DOWN

PRODUCED by The Who with associate producer Glyn Johns, at Olympic Studios, Barnes, on June 6, 1972. An upbeat *Lifehouse* outtake with a slow synthesizer break, this track falls short of the standards reached by any of the *Who's Next* songs, though the message – a diatribe about the lack of relationship between artist and audience – comes across clearly enough. This track remained uncompleted until 1974 when Roger finally finished the vocal so it could be included on *Odds & Sods*.

LITTLE BILLY

ORIGINAL recording produced by Kit Lambert at IBC Studios, London, on February 11, 1968, and mixed at Gold Star Studios, Hollywood, February 26,1968,

'Little Billy' is a stern anti-smoking song The Who recorded on behalf of the American Cancer Society, with fairly grisly lyrics – for once Pete might have been inspired by John – that really do suggest that smoking can kill. Considering that

all four members of The Who were heavy smokers at this time, it was somewhat hypocritical but it's an entertaining narrative piece, which the ACS declined to use on the grounds that it was too morbid. With the change in attitudes towards cigarette smoking in the 21st Century, perhaps it's ripe for a re-release.

TOO MUCH OF ANYTHING

SEE *Who's Next* bonus tracks.

GLOW GIRL

THE ORIGINAL recording was produced by Kit Lambert at De Lane Lea Studios, London, in January 1968, and within it lie the seeds of *Tommy*: it closes with the opening lines from 'It's A Boy', albeit referring to a girl..."It's a girl Mrs Walker..."

Pete: "I wrote it because we were taking off in a plane which I seriously thought was going to crash, and as I was going up I was writing this list. I thought that if I was a chick and I was in a plane that was diving for the ground and I had my boyfriend next to me and we were on our honeymoon or we were about to get married, I know what I'd think of. I'd think about him and I'd think about what I am going to be missing. So I went through this list... of what was in the chick's purse – cigarettes, Tampax – a whole lyrical list and then holding his hand and what he felt and was gonna say to her.

"He is a romanticist... he is trying to have some romantic and soaring last thoughts. Eventually what happens is they crash and they are reincarnated that instant musically... they've been reincarnated as this girl. 'It's a girl, Mrs Walker, it's a girl,' – that was supposed to be the end of the thing."

As it happened, it was merely the beginning of far greater things.

See also *Who Sell Out* bonus tracks.

PURE AND EASY

THIS IS THE version produced by The Who, and associate producer Glyn Johns, at Olympic Studios, London, in May 1971.

See *Who's Next* bonus tracks.

FAITH IN SOMETHING BIGGER

THIS EARLY, unsophisticated (even for 1968) attempt by Pete to express his growing devotion to Him was produced by Kit Lambert at CBS Studios, London, on January 4, 1968. It has charming, albeit unsubtle, vocal harmonies, and by The Who's own standards, is rather naïve.

Pete: "God, this is embarrassing. I don't know where to hide. Well I mean the whole thing about 'Him' is that 'He' is everywhere, isn't 'He'? A modest beginning to the musico-

spiritual work on the irreligious Who. The guitar solo is the worst I've ever heard. They're great lads, the rest of the boys in the band. Do you think anybody else would put up with this nonsense? Anyway, the whole idea is preposterous, something, something bigger than 'Us? Us! The Who!' A quick listen to this lads will bring us quickly down to size I can assure you."

I'M THE FACE
(Meaden)

'I'M THE Face' was the first record released by The Who, or The High Numbers as they were then called, on July 3, 1964. A Mod rallying cry with lyrics by their then manager Pete Meaden set to the melody of Slim Harpo's 'Got Love If You Want It', it failed to make the charts. The original single on the Fontana label, however, has since become – along with *Who Did It** – the most valuable collectors' item in the band's entire UK catalogue. A mint condition copy could set you back almost £300. Rumour has it that only 1,000 copies were pressed, and that a quantity of them were apparently bought up by Meaden in a chart fix.

Forty years on 'I'm The Face' rocks out with all the raw enthusiasm of a teenage band on the first rung of the pop ladder, and although Keith is subdued by later standards, John and Pete display embryonic Who tendencies behind Roger's giddy shout. This becomes patently obvious on the remixed and remastered CD.

[* *Who Did It* featured side one from *A Quick One* and side two from *The Who Sell Out* and was briefly available via mail order from Track Records.]

NAKED EYE

THIS IS first studio version of the song, produced by Pete at Eel Pie during the spring of 1970. See *Who's Next* bonus tracks.

LONG LIVE ROCK

THIS FULL tilt rocker was produced by The Who with Glyn Johns at Olympic Studios, London, on June 5, 1972. It was released as a UK single on April 1, 1979, reaching Number 48, and as a US single in June 1979.

'Long Live Rock' was originally written as part of an album about the history of The Who, a concept that Pete abandoned in favour of *Quadrophenia*. It first appeared in the film *That'll Be The Day*, featuring Keith Moon, and was sung by Billy Fury. Reminiscent of Fifties style rock and roll with jangly piano and almost-12-bar arrangements, Pete sings lead and makes several sideways references to headline-grabbing aspects of The Who's story. A fine rocker; whoever said that Keith couldn't keep proper time should listen hard to this one.

Remixed and Remastered CD

THIS CONSISTED OF A SINGLE DISC BUT EXPANDED BY 12 BONUS TRACKS. The intent was to make a number of compilations redundant while keeping with the original spirit of collecting together various Who curios. With the large number of bonus tracks possible on the CD format, the original sequence was changed to follow the chronological order of recording.

I'M THE FACE
(Meaden)

'I'M THE Face' was part of the original *Odds & Sods* in 1974, and the remixed version here first appeared on The Who's box set, *30 Years Of Maximum R&B*, released in 1994.

LEAVING HERE
(Holland/Dozier/Holland)

THIS AND the track that follows were produced by Shel Talmy, recorded circa February-March 1965 at Pye Studios, and were previously unreleased as of 1998.

A double sided acetate of these tracks, probably the only one in existence, was acquired by Phil Hopkins, a keen Who collector and co-publisher at the fanzine *Generations.* "It was given to me by a chap who bought it for next to nothing in a car boot sale," says Hopkins. "He didn't want to profit from it... just to make sure it found a proper home."

Supposedly another, earlier, version of this song was produced by Chris Parmeinter at Fontana Studios, when The Who were The High Numbers, but has yet to surface, if indeed it exists.

BABY DON'T YOU DO IT
(Holland/Dozier/Holland)

THE REVERSE side of the acetate disc, this is the earliest known version of The Who performing the Tamla Motown song recorded by Marvin Gaye in 1964 that would become a stage favourite in the early Seventies. A live version of this number (See *Rarities Vol 2* in Compilations) first appeared as the B-side of 'Join Together' in 1972.

SUMMERTIME BLUES
(Cochran/Capehart)

RECORDED at De Lane Lea Studios, London, on October 10, 1967, this previously unreleased studio version of 'Summertime Blues' was originally recorded as part of a session leased to the BBC. The Who – as The Detours – had been playing the song since before Keith Moon joined the band in 1964, and of course, recorded their definitive live version on 1970's *Live At Leeds*.

UNDER MY THUMB
(Jagger/Richards)

PRODUCED by Kit Lambert at De Lane Lea Studios, London, on June 28, 1967, this early mix of the take, released as the B-side to 'The Last Time' in the UK on June 30, 1967), is pre the overdubs of Pete's bass riff and fuzz box lead guitar. (See *Rarities Vol. 1* in Compilations for the best CD source for the version as it was originally released.) It also has a longer fadeout.

The Who recorded two Rolling Stones' songs as a gesture of support for Mick Jagger and Keith Richards who were facing imprisonment on drug charges. It was the Who's intention to continue recording Stones' songs as long as Jagger and Richards were in jail. Mick and Keith had the gall to win release before The Who had a chance to record any more. Pete played bass because John Entwistle was away on his honeymoon.

MARY ANNE WITH THE SHAKY HAND

PREVIOUSLY unreleased prior to 1998, this is an alternate mix of the electric version of 'Mary Anne...' released as the US B-side to 'I Can See For Miles' in September 1967. Al Kooper's organ fills, mixed out or low on the released take, are more prominent here and the track ends instead of fading. Recorded in New York at Mirasound Studios on August 6, 1967. See also *The Who Sell Out* CD Bonus Tracks and *Rarities Vol. 1*.

MY WAY
(Cochran)

RECORDED at De Lane Lea Studios, London, on October 10, 1967 as part of a session for the BBC. Previously unreleased as of 1998. The Who featured this number in their stage act during their Detours days, and occasionally played it live during 1967 and 1968.

FAITH IN SOMETHING BIGGER

FROM THE original *Odds & Sods* album.

GLOW GIRL

FROM THE original *Odds & Sods* album and a bonus track on the 1995 CD re-issue of *The Who Sell Out*.

LITTLE BILLY

FROM THE original *Odds & Sods* album, and included on the *30 Years Of Maximum R&B* box set in 1994.

YOUNG MAN BLUES
(Allison)

PRODUCED by Kit Lambert during the early Tommy sessions at IBC Studios, London, in September or October 1968, this studio version of 'Young Man Blues' was intended to be that as released on the long unavailable UK 1969 Track sampler album, *The House That Track Built*. To the delight of collectors, it proved to be a previously unknown, albeit inferior slower version. The Who's better-known (live) version appeared on 1970's *Live At Leeds*. See also *Tommy* Deluxe Edition CD.

COUSIN KEVIN MODEL CHILD

THIS WAS later included on the *Tommy* Deluxe Edition bonus disc (2003).

LOVE AIN'T FOR KEEPING

RECORDED during the Record Plant, New York *Lifehouse* sessions in March 1971. Previously unreleased prior to 1998 but later included on *Who's Next* Deluxe Edition (2003).

TIME IS PASSING

RECORDED at Olympic Studios, London in May/June 1971, during the *Who's Next* sessions, this is the Who version of a song previously available as a track on Pete's first official solo album *Who Came First* (September 1972). This mono version was remastered from a damaged master tape.

PURE AND EASY

FROM THE original *Odds & Sods* album.

TOO MUCH OF ANYTHING

FROM THE original *Odds & Sods* album.

LONG LIVE ROCK

FROM THE original *Odds & Sods* album.

PUT THE MONEY DOWN

FROM THE original *Odds & Sods* album.

WE CLOSE TONIGHT

PREVIOUSLY unreleased prior to 1998, this outtake from *Quadrophenia* was recorded on Ronnie Lane's Mobile studio on June 20, 1973. Unusually it features John singing a song written by Pete, about a Joker James-character telling lies to impress a prospective date, with speeded up vocals from Keith – halfway to chipmunks!

POSTCARD

FROM THE original *Odds & Sods* album.

NOW I'M A FARMER

FROM THE original *Odds & Sods* album.

WATER

THIS IS the studio version of the song produced by Pete at Eel Pie Studios during the spring of 1970. See also *Who's Next* bonus tracks

NAKED EYE

THIS IS the version recorded at Eel Pie Studio in spring 1970. From the original *Odds & Sods* album. See also *Who's Next* bonus tracks.

Tommy Soundtrack

Original UK issue: Polydor 2657 014, released March 1975;
UK CD: Polydor 841 121-2, remastered Polydor 841 121-2, 2001
US: Polydor PD2-9505 released March 1975;
CD: Polydor 841 121-2, remastered Polydor 422 841 121-2, 2001

NOT STRICTLY A WHO ALBUM, THOUGH ALL FOUR MEMBERS OF THE WHO are featured on the reworked versions of *Tommy* songs as they appeared in the movie. There's an interesting selection of vocalists, including Oliver Reed (whose singing voice makes Keith sound like a choirboy), Jack Nicholson (who couldn't sing either), Tina Turner (her 'Acid Queen' is terrific), Ann-Margret and Elton John, whose spin through 'Pinball Wizard' with his own stage band is the album's highlight and which became a hit single in 1975.

By and large, the songs all feature an abundance of Pete's synthesizer work and elaborate choral arrangements by backing vocalists brought in to offset the musical shortcomings of tone-deaf actors. Several songs are radically reworked by the all-star band (which, ironically, included Kenney Jones drumming on many of the tracks since Keith was absent), and there are a couple of completely new songs in 'Champagne' and 'Mother And Son'. John does most of the bass work as well as playing all the horn parts. Pete played the synthesizers and also produced the musical score, a thankless chore – in retrospect – that drove him to the brink of another nervous breakdown.

This soundtrack is really a kitsch novelty item of interest only to Who academics. Stick to The Who's original version, or better still, seek out live versions of *Tommy* material by The Who circa 1969/70.

The Who By Numbers

Original UK issue: Polydor 2490 129, released October 1975;
CD: Polydor 831 522-2, remixed and remastered Polydor 533 844-2, 1996
US: MCA 2161, released October 1975;
CD: MCA MCAD-37002, remixed and remastered MCAD-11493, 1996

BY THE TIME THE GROUP GOT AROUND TO RECORDING *THE WHO BY NUMBERS*, they were tired, insecure and feeling the pace, and although this record was never intended as a concept album, there is a running theme of discontent, disillusionment and, above all, the dilemma of growing old in the band that once sang about hoping to die first. It was almost as if Pete approached this stage in The Who's career as a penitent might approach the confession box. Never one to shrink from the truth, Pete lays bare his soul and the demons that lay within, and it didn't always make for easy listening.

Overall, this release has a much lighter sound than any of its predecessors. Here Townshend abandons the synthesizers of *Who's Next* and *Quadrophenia*, and eschews his trademark block chords for diligent lead guitar. Keith's drums rarely pound as they once did and Roger's voice, becoming deeper but more sonorous as it aged, no longer spits out Townshend's words with the ferocity of old. Only John retains his trademark bass-style, fast and fluid and, on 'Dreaming From The Waist', in a class of his own.

At this point in their career The Who on record and The Who live became two different entities. Only two of the new songs here – 'Squeeze Box' and 'Dreaming From The Waist' – were played with any regularity in a live set that gradually became a celebratory and vigorously performed parade of former glories, though 'Slip Kid' and 'However Much I Booze' were tried on stage and soon discarded. On its release The Who made a triumphant return to the stage, touring the US with the same zest and expertise that they showed five years earlier, but deep inside Townshend knew that to survive as a creative vehicle, and therefore retain his interest, The Who had to change – or stagnate. The problem was finding the direction in which to change while meeting the expectations of fans who liked their Who loud and brash, just as they always had been.

All of these factors produced a rather non-Who sounding Who album, or perhaps more accurately, a Pete Townshend solo album using the Who as a back up reference. Thought of in that light, the album has much to recommend it: 'Slip Kid', 'Dreaming From The Waist' and 'Imagine A Man' were all first rate songs, 'Success Story' was good enough to have succeeded 'My Wife' as a stage vehicle for John, 'Squeeze Box' was fun, and 'Blue, Red And Grey' was as charming a solo piece as Pete has ever recorded. The album has aged well, it just doesn't have that 'kick in the gut' effect of earlier Who albums.

Clad in a self-depreciatory join-up-the-dots cartoon design by John, it reached Number 7 in UK and 8 in the US.

SLIP KID

AN EIGHT-BEAT count-in leads into a shuffle rhythm that could be a drum machine, before Roger and Pete swap autobiographical lines about a rock 'n'roll kid who's lost when he grows up. With Roger singing, "There's no easy way to be free", and Pete rejoining "It's a hard, hard world", the mood of the album is immediately apparent. Nicky Hopkins is featured on piano and there's a fine guitar solo.

HOWEVER MUCH I BOOZE

ONE OF the distinctive aspects of *The Who By Numbers* is that songs of personal anguish are couched in pleasant, almost cheerful melodies. Here, while Pete sings lyrics about his failures and vanities, reaching the conclusion that, "There ain't no way out", the band skips along lightly and Pete adds some authentic country style picking during his solo. The short, slow middle-eight is charmingly sung.

SQUEEZE BOX

AN uncharacteristically jolly song with lascivious undertones,

'Squeeze Box' is a most un-Who-like tumble into uncomplicated rolling rhythms enlivened by Pete as multi-instrumentalist on accordion and banjo as well as guitar, though the ending, with the tremolo chord, is classic Who. 'Squeeze Box' became a minor hit single, reaching Number 10 in the UK and 16 in the US, followed by some pretty interesting covers by artists such as Freddy Fender and Laura Branigan.

Pete: "I went out and bought an accordion and learned to play it in about ten minutes, so it's a devastatingly simple song."

DREAMING FROM THE WAIST

PETE HAS said he hated playing this track, mainly because of the tricky opening chords high up on the fretboard, but with its tumbling rhythm, melodic, harmony-clad chorus and general sizzle, it ranks with many of The Who's best ever songs. It also offers John an opportunity to stretch out: his popping bass solo in the closing bars is a stunning display of virtuosity which he'd play live with the casual aplomb of the player whose fingers other bassists would kill for.

IMAGINE A MAN

WITH AN introduction not unlike 'Behind Blue Eyes', 'Imagine A Man' is a dramatic ballad with a lovely, distinctive melody and profound lyrics about the tedium of day-to-day life, something that rock stars are not supposed to know much about. Townshend kept in touch with the street more than most, however, and his observations are keenly felt.

SUCCESS STORY
(Entwistle)

THE MALAISE that affected Pete had its effect on John as well, for the message of this catchy autobiographical rocker seems to be that being a member of The Who used to be fun but no longer. John's songs rarely slotted into whatever theme occupied Pete's mind when The Who were recording, but this time he was spot on. "I may go far if I... smash my guitar", can only have been written about Townshend. John contributes a great hook line throughout.

THEY ARE ALL IN LOVE

THE LIGHTEST – and prettiest – song on the album again speaks of disillusionment and cynicism, with a melodious Roger and gentle piano from Nicky Hopkins disguising bitter sentiments about the music industry.

Pete: "The song was about what the band has become. It was about money, about law courts, about lawyers and accountants. Those things had never mattered and then the band had a backlog of tax problems and unpaid royalties. We had to deal with it. I really felt like crawling off and dying."

BLUE RED AND GREY

IN WHICH Pete, accompanying himself on ukulele and unsupported by the rest of the band, declaims the millionaire lifestyle in favour of the virtues of a simple life. An uncomplicated melody, performed with the kind of tongue-in-cheek sincerity that Pete had previously demonstrated on his first solo album *Who Came First*. The silver band adds to the sense of poignancy. Utterly charming.

HOW MANY FRIENDS

SURROUNDED by sycophants who never say what they really mean, Pete's misery knows no bounds but as Dave Marsh observed in his Who biography, *Before I Get Old*, Townshend probably enjoyed the company of fewer sycophants and yesmen than most rock stars, and many of his oldest friends who stuck around were as outspoken as he was. Of course, the same could not be said for Keith who attracted legions of hangers-on that laughed like trained hyenas every time the hapless drummer opened his mouth.

Roger takes the vocals on a bitter, piano-based song.

IN A HAND OR A FACE

WITH Roger sounding as bitter as ever in a final slab of self-pity, this song is pinned together by a repetitive three chord riff, but it's musically inadequate to hold up as the album's closer, sounding rather anonymous and highlighted only by Pete's lively solo and a brief drum break. Because of the quality of production compared to the rest of the album, this song appears to have been slapped on to end the album almost as an afterthought.

Remixed and Remastered CD

SQUEEZE BOX (LIVE)

RECORDED live at Swansea Football Ground on June 12, 1976. Previously unreleased as of 1996.

BEHIND BLUE EYES (LIVE)

RECORDED live at Swansea Football Ground on June 12, 1976. Previously unreleased as of 1996.

DREAMING FROM THE WAIST (LIVE)

RECORDED live at Swansea Football Ground on June 12, 1976. Previously available on the 1994 box set *Thirty Years Of Maximum R&B*. The Who performed the song faultlessly, especially the vocal harmonies on the verses and John's immaculate bass solo towards the end gained enormously when played live.

Who Are You

Original UK issue: Polydor 2490 147 WHOD 5004, released August 1978;
CD: Polydor 831 557-2, remixed and remastered Polydor 533 845-2, 1996
US: MCA 3050, released August 1978; CD: MCA MCAD-37003; MFSL
UDCD 561 (Gold Disc), remixed and remastered MCA MCAD-11492, 1996

INERTIA NEVER SUITED THE WHO. THEY THRIVED ON FAST PACED ENERGY AND produced their best work on the run. Three years between the release of *The Who By Numbers* and *Who Are You* was the longest gap ever between Who releases and in the meantime much had occurred, none of it beneficial to the group. Never the closest of colleagues outside of the recording studio and the stage, during these three years the band members had grown apart in so many ways that they no longer resembled anything remotely like the gang they'd once been. Pete's spiritual and intellectual quests were ongoing but frustrating, and his musings were quite alien to Roger, the practical landowner who just wanted to get on with his job and not philosophise about it; John was simply a very skilled professional musician who wanted and needed to work regularly; Keith, his marriage now over, was sick with alcoholism, lonely and desperate for something besides the disintegrating Who to fill an empty life.

Pete knew that the only way the group could survive was to steer them in new directions. The other three resisted the insecurity of change. Given half the chance, Pete would have broken up the group before *Who Are You* was recorded, but he felt a loyalty to his three colleagues, especially Keith, and soldiered on regardless. The result is a transitional album based largely around synthesizer patterns that could have pointed the way to the future were it not for Keith dying within a month of its release. In a stylistic shift that would become more apparent later, the arrangements of the songs – and the songs themselves – are more complex than ever before, and they tend to meander where once they would have been blunt and to the point. As would also become the pattern in future, John's songs take greater prominence, and Roger sings an Entwistle song.

Moon's accidental, but tragically predictable death on September 7, 1978 completely overshadowed the album's release. Ironically, he is photographed on the cover sitting on a chair with the words 'Not To Be Taken Away' on its back; the other irony is that on one song, 'Music Must Change', Keith didn't play drums because he couldn't handle its unusual tempo. "But I'm the best Keith Moon style drummer in the world," he is reported to have told Pete when he couldn't play it. Moon wasn't firing on all cylinders throughout the recording and it shows, but perhaps this is what Pete might have wanted. Moon, more than any of his three colleagues, represented the thundering recklessness of the old – and younger–style Who.

Although Keith's death freed them from the grip of the past, the future, as the final two albums demonstrated, turned out to be a barren land all the same, creatively at least. *Who Are You* reached Number 6 in UK and 2 in US.

NEW SONG

WITH THE synthesizer as the dominant instrument throughout the album, it's appropriate that this should open as the first song, an upbeat, unconventional sounding rocker that bemoans the repetitive nature of rock as a whole and The Who in particular. "We sing the same old song," sings Roger but with less cynicism than on the previous album. That the song tends to drag can be put down to Keith's lack of energy, a sad state of affairs that was never truly remedied.

HAD ENOUGH
(Entwistle)

THE FIRST of two John Entwistle songs written for a science fiction fantasy that was originally intended to become a solo album. Here it is sung by Roger and dominated by synthesizer, from the intro to the maudlin sweeping strings in the solo that sound rather like the soundtrack to an epic western. There's also a brass interlude from John, and Roger's vocals on the chorus are eminently listenable.

905
(Entwistle)

THE SECOND sci-fi fantasy song, carried forth by a bip-bopping synthesiszer that features John singing the autobiography of a robot, but it's lost in the drabness of the tune.

SISTER DISCO

SYNTHESIZERS again dominate this fairly well-known upbeat rocker sung by Roger, which has little to do with disco music but more to do with fans, a subject Pete is drawn to again and again. As ever Pete comes in to sing a slower middle-eight, and he contributes some nice picking in the solo and chord work at the end. 'Sister Disco' became a popular stage number for the new-look Who that emerged after Keith Moon's death.

MUSIC MUST CHANGE

KEITH WAS unable to play the tricky time signature on this track, which isn't surprising as it's no foot tapper. It meanders through verses at a shuffle, then breaks out into experimental jazz tempos of uncharacteristic complexity for The Who. Roger also sings a softer refrain at odds with the verses. The message here is heartfelt: Pete wanted music to change as much as the punk rockers, but any punk listening to this elaborate piece of art rock would have thrown up within seconds!

TRICK OF THE LIGHT
(Entwistle)

JOHN'S multi-stringed bass dominates an uptempo song about a night with a prostitute to the extent that everyone and everything else in the studio is pretty superfluous. Murky stuff, and it now serves as an unpleasant reminder of John's final visit to Las Vegas.

GUITAR AND PEN

ANOTHER experimental song with Roger's vocals on the operatic side and the unison chorus sounding vaguely like the chorus line from a Gilbert & Sullivan comic opera. Midway through, the song descends into a free-form solo and it's clear that this is the kind of material Pete enjoyed writing at the time, whether The Who liked it or not. I doubt whether Keith did. The US MFSL 'Gold' CD contains an alternative version, even more mannered than this cut.

There's a better example of this

type of Pete's writing style called 'Street In The City' on *Rough Mix*, the album that Pete recorded with Ronnie Lane in 1976/77. Indeed, *Rough Mix* contains at least two Townshend songs, 'My Baby Gives It Away' and 'Keep Me Turning', which are better than almost all the material that Pete recorded with The Who from this point onwards.

LOVE IS COMING DOWN

A SLOW BALLAD with a rather slushy MOR string arrangement swells up on the choruses but goes nowhere in particular.

WHO ARE YOU

ONE DAY in January 1977 Pete spent more hours than he cared to remember in a meeting to sort out The Who's tangled financial affairs, and came away with a cheque for seven figures. Most people would have been delighted at this outcome, but Pete was disgusted with himself. He was a musician, not a businessman. So he got drunk as hell at The Speakeasy, the London rockbiz club, where he encountered two of The Sex Pistols who pronounced themselves Who fans. This only aggrieved Pete more, so he tore up the cheque. When he left the club he was pie-eyed, and he slumped into a doorway, where he spent the night. At dawn, he was awoken by a policeman, who recognised Townshend and sent him on his way. Reaching home in Twickenham, his wife Karen was waiting for him. "Where have you been?!" she asked. "I've been to hell and back," Pete groaned through his hangover. This story forms the lyrical basis for 'Who Are You'.

The musical basis is the lengthy prologue, mid-section, and close, in which the title is repeated in a looping synthesizer-propelled chant similar to that used by middle eastern Sufi dancers as they near a trancelike state. Although it ebbs and flows, and at one point Pete plays an acoustic refrain, it embodies all the energy of past Who classics and at over six minutes is far and away the most arresting track on the album. Even Keith manages to keep up the tempo on this one.

Roger ad-libs "Who the fuck are you" and, when performed in concert, demonstrated his physical fitness by running on the spot for what seemed like ages. Although its message is unclear, 'Who Are You' is unquestionably the last great Who song recorded by the original group.

Bonus Tracks on Remastered CD

NO ROAD ROMANCE

RECORDED at Pete's Eel Pie Studio, Goring, Berkshire, April 1978. This is a Pete demo, featuring piano, fretless bass, drums, and vocals, for a song brought to the *Who Are You* sessions that was deemed surplus to requirements. Previously unreleased prior to 1996. (The tape dropout on the first verse is present on the analog master.)

EMPTY GLASS

RECORDED at Ramport Studio, Battersea, April 1978. this was originally titled, 'Choirboy', and is The Who's rough mix of the song that eventually became the title track to Pete's 1980 solo album. It features John and Keith playing over one of Pete's demos. Note the acoustic guitar and John's unusual bass harmonics in the introduction. Previously unreleased prior to 1996.

GUITAR AND PEN (OLYMPIC '78 MIX)

THIS IS an alternative mix, with a more aggressive guitar track, recorded by Glyn Johns and Jon Astley in May 1978. It was rejected in favour of the Ramport mix that appeared on the album. Previously unreleased prior to 1996.

LOVE IS COMING DOWN
(WORK-IN-PROGRESS MIX)

THIS VERSION of the song features different piano and bass parts, and has only a guide vocal. Previously unreleased prior to 1996.

WHO ARE YOU
(LOST VERSE MIX)

THIS VERSION of the song features different lyrics in the second verse, which Pete later re-wrote. Previously unreleased prior to 1996.

The Kids Are Alright

Original UK issue: Polydor 2675 179, released June 1979;
CD: Polydor 517 947-2 (edited version), remastered and restored
Polydor 543 694-2, 2001 US: MCA2 11005, released June 1979;
CD: MCA MCAD-6899 (edited version),
remastered and restored MCA 314 543 694-2, 2001

THE DOUBLE SOUNDTRACK FOR *THE KIDS ARE ALRIGHT* CONTAINS MATERIAL that doesn't actually appear in the film, while the film contains material that doesn't appear on the soundtrack. To make things more confusing, the original CD issues edited what had been the fourth side of the vinyl album due to then existing technical limitations. Certain tracks were identical to the original releases, which in the movie The Who lip-synched to playback.

The soundtrack, taken from various film clips, regular releases and special staged performances, was remixed by John Entwistle. It offered alternate versions of previously released material, mainly live cuts, many of which, especially 'Sparks', 'See Me Feel Me', 'Baba O'Riley' and 'Won't Get Fooled Again', were exceptionally well performed considering the circumstances. Whether the performances are the definitive takes of The Who live is open to question.

The album and restored CD track listing is as follows:

SIDE ONE: 'My Generation', from *The Smothers Brothers Comedy Hour* TV show, September 15, 1967; 'I Can't Explain', from *Shindig!* TV show, August 3, 1965; 'Happy Jack' (not in the film), recorded live at Leeds University, February 14, 1970; 'I Can See For Miles' (not in film), from *The Smothers Brothers Comedy Hour* TV show, September 15, 1967; 'Magic Bus' (regular studio version), from *Beat Club* German TV, October 7, 1968; 'Long Live Rock' (regular studio version), June 5, 1972;

SIDE TWO: 'Anyway Anyhow Anywhere', from *Ready Steady Go!*, July 1, 1965; 'Young Man Blues', from the London Coliseum, December 14, 1969; 'My Wife' (not in film) live from Kilburn State Theatre, London, December 15, 1977; 'Baba O'Riley', live from Shepperton Studios, May 25, 1978;

SIDE THREE: 'A Quick One (While He's Away)', live from T*he Rolling Stones Rock & Roll Circus*, December 11, 1968; 'Tommy Can You Hear Me' (regular studio version), from *Beat Club* German TV, August 26 & 28, 1969; 'Sparks', live from Woodstock, August 17, 1969; 'Pinball Wizard', live from Woodstock, August 17, 1969; 'See Me, Feel Me', live from Woodstock, August 17, 1969;

SIDE FOUR: 'Join Together', 'Road Runner', 'My Generation Blues', live from Pontiac Silverdome, Michigan, December 6, 1975; 'Won't Get Fooled Again', live from Shepperton Studios, May 25, 1978.

The Kids Are Alright reached Number 26 in UK Number 8 in US.

Quadrophenia
Soundtrack

Original UK issue: Polydor 2625 037, released September 1979;
CD: Polydor 519 999-2 (Edited version),
remastered and restored Polydor 543 611-4, 2001
US: Polydor PD2-6235, released September 1979;
CD: Polydor 314 519 999-2 (Edited version),
remastered and restored Polydor 314 519 691-2, 2001

THE SOUNDTRACK TO THE FILM *QUADROPHENIA* **WAS A DOUBLE ALBUM** that included a selection of tracks remixed from the original double album by John Entwistle, three 'new' Who songs not on the original Who LP, 'Zoot Suit' by The High Numbers, and a fourth side of music by various artists used in the film. This was deleted from the original CD but has been restored on the current issues.

ZOOT SUIT
(Meaden)

THE B-SIDE of 'I'm The Face' is actually the melody of an obscure US soul song with new lyrics by Pete Meaden designed to appeal to The Who's Mod following. The High Numbers take the song at a cracking pace, Pete sounds like a jazz guitarist and Roger's vocals are answered by the band, Merseybeat style. As in all The High Numbers tracks, Keith's drums are mixed too low.

ents are chucking him out of the family home – but on record it's more than a tad tedious. Obviously written to accompany the onscreen action.

FOUR FACES

WITH PETE on vocals backed by his own piano, this song finds Jimmy pondering his quadraphonic personality after being thrown out. Pleasant and tuneful but lightweight compared to the real *Quadrophenia* material.

GET OUT AND STAY OUT

WITH THE title line repeated endlessly, this track makes its point in the movie – Jimmy's par-

JOKER JAMES

AN ODD little song about James the practical joker whose odd sense of humour costs him girlfriend after girlfriend when he inflicts on them the joys of whoopee cushions and itching powder. If Pete wasn't credited with writing this, most Who watchers would swear it was an Entwistle song, at least judging by the lyrics.

Face Dances

Original UK issue: Polydor 2302 106 WHOD 5037, released March 1981;
CD: Polydor 517 948-2, remixed and remastered Polydor 537 695-2, 1997
US: Warner Bros (WB) HS 3516, released March 1981;
CD: WB: 3516-2; reissued MCA MCAD 25-25987, MFSL 1-115,
remixed and remastered MCA MCAD-11634, 1997

AFTER KEITH'S DEATH THE WHO BECAME A DIFFERENT BAND AND THE TWO albums they made with Kenney Jones on drums reflect that. The greatest difference is what appears to be a lack of direction – even a lack of conviction; but the blame for this cannot be laid at Jones' feet. Pete was no longer saving his best material for The Who – his solo albums took preference – and the songs he now offered Roger seemed too wordy, too autobiographical, and altogether unsuited to Daltrey's style of singing. Additionally, Pete's melodies were complex, often convoluted and introverted, far removed from simple rock melodies that directly touch the emotions. The new songs relied more heavily on keyboards, a most un-Who-like development.

The Who sounded familiar only on John Entwistle's songs, but with a leaden, lumpy kind of heavy-metal sound, lacking interesting melodies and quite unlike the springy, alert sound of the best rock songs that Pete – and occasionally John – had written previously. On Pete's, the music was light and the words often seem out of sync, while John's contributions sounded like another band altogether. It's safe to say, the results puzzled old fans and failed to capture new ones.

Although Keith's drumming had deteriorated on the final Who album, his peculiar up-front style was sorely missed. He contributed an integral part to The Who's unique sound that helped drive the melody along on many of the best songs. In contrast, Jones was a steady, on the beat timekeeper, eminently professional by anyone's standards, but these abilities were not in line with The Who's glorious past and never would be. Now The Who were just another rock band, indeed a very good one live, but no longer did they stand out from the pack, at least not on record.

John summed up the situation better than anyone: "The last two Who albums are a kind of blank. By the time we were recording them personalities were clashing. There were different ideas of music policy. General backbiting. People not agreeing with each other. Roger and Pete always had differing opinions about everything, but myself and Keith would make our minds up and, usually, things went in the way that myself and Keith wanted, so we never got into four-piece arguments usually. After Keith died, those were the hardest times..."

Face Dances, produced by Eagles producer Bill Szymczyk, was released at a time when the new look Who launched themselves in a barrage of publicity, which probably explains why it leapt to Number 2 in the UK album charts and Number 4 in the US. The band toured excessively (particularly the States) in the two years following Jones' arrival, but the show they presented relied almost entirely on past glories. When they played material from *Face Dances*, many fans took the opportunity to take a break. Aside from Jones, there were other changes in the traditional Who modus operandi: John 'Rabbit' Bundrick (ex-Free, Crawler) played keyboards on stage and played them well, and on some of the newer numbers Roger played guitar on stage for the first time since the days of The Detours in 1963.

Incidentally, The Who never released their version of Pete's song, 'Face Dances'. Pete re-recorded it for his *All the Best Cowboys Have Chinese Eyes* solo album (1982). A shame as it's better than almost anything on this album.

YOU BETTER YOU BET

THE BEST known song on the album, the one that was deservedly chosen for a single, and has pleasantly developed into an exciting highlight performed live. 'You Better You Bet' opens with a popping synthesizer line and features several Who trademarks: changes in tempo, rumbling bass runs and some powerful upfront singing from Roger who is clearly responding well to the challenge of a Moon-less band. Indeed, Roger's accent sounds more like that of the traditional Londoner he is than ever.

The best track on *Faces Dances* by a country mile, it reached Number 9 in the UK singles charts.

DON'T LET GO THE COAT

OPENING with a riff that sounds like an American AOR band, 'Don't Let Go The Coat' switches between a gentle rolling rhythm, and a tempo that for The Who could almost be described as funky. Neither sounds like The Who of old and Roger struggles with a lyric inspired by Meher Baba's instructions to his followers not to abandon his 'robe', an allegory for his teachings. But the singer seems to be apologising for his inadequacy and unworthiness, which doesn't suit Roger's braggadocio style.

CACHE CACHE

SIMILAR in tempo to 'You Better You Bet' but lacking the energy and veering off at slower tangents, this is a rather dull song with curious lyrics inspired by a nocturnal drunken visit to the Berlin Zoo which saw Pete join the bears in their cage. Lifted by a great guitar solo, but still lacklustre and, even with a lyric sheet, difficult to comprehend.

THE QUIET ONE
(Entwistle)

"STILL WATERS run deep" according to this autobiographical slab of heavy metal sung in a raucous but rather tuneless tone by John after smoking several packs of Marlboros. This rocks along with the balls of 'My Wife' but without the interesting changes or power chords. John often sang this on stage following the album's release.

DID YOU STEAL MY MONEY?

AN UNTYPICAL jerky time signature dominates an undistinguished tune in which the title is repeated too many times for comfort. Forgettable.

HOW CAN YOU DO IT ALONE?

PETE Townshend might have written rock operas but he was never known for writing confessional story songs, at least not until this stage in his career. 'How Can You Do It Alone?' certainly contains the most interesting lyrics on *Face Dances*, set to a slap-bang tempo. It's about life's down-and-outs, as encountered by Pete, but the complexities of the verses are again incompatible with Roger's vocal style and the message of the song – show sympathy for losers – gets lost in the elaborate arrangement. The peculiar martial rhythm in the middle doesn't help either.

DAILY RECORDS

ANOTHER autobiographical song about ageing and trying to keep up with musical fashion that just doesn't suit Roger's voice and, apart from the great jangly guitar solo, lacks conviction as a result.

YOU
(Entwistle)

ROGER sings John's second HM-style contribution, a song about a reluctant Romeo anxious to avoid further entanglements in case the consequences prove as expensive as previous affairs. Fast and furious, like 'The Quiet One', and enlivened in part by John's riffing on what sounds like an eight-string bass guitar.

ANOTHER TRICKY DAY

'ANOTHER Tricky Day' closes the album on a lyrically pessimistic note, although the song itself is more interesting than most on *Face Dances* and was played live on the tours that followed.

Bonus Tracks on Remastered CD

I LIKE NIGHTMARES

THIS SONG was worked on during the sessions for *Face Dances* but left off the final recording. Previously unreleased prior to 1997.

IT'S IN YOU

SEE ABOVE.

SOMEBODY SAVED ME

SEE ABOVE. Pete subsequently re-recorded this song for release on his *All The Best Cowboys Have Chinese Eyes* album in 1982.

HOW CAN YOU DO IT ALONE?

LIVE International Amphitheatre, Chicago, December 8, 1979. This jam became the song that appeared on the album. Previously unreleased prior to 1997.

THE QUIET ONE

LIVE FROM Shea Stadium, New York, on October 13, 1982, the second of two live shows by The Who at the same New York venue. Previously unreleased prior to 1997.

It's Hard

Original UK issue: Polydor WHOD 5066, released September 1982;
CD: Polydor 800 106-2, remixed and remastered
Polydor 537 696-2, 1997
US: Warner Bros WB 23731, released September 1982;
CD: Warner Bros (WB) 23731-2, reissued MCA MCAD-25986,
remixed and remastered MCA MCAD-11635, 1997

IT'S DIFFICULT TO GET AWAY FROM THE NOTION THAT THE WHO'S FINAL ALBUM was recorded purely as a contractual obligation to keep a substantial advance that otherwise would have had to be returned to the band's American record company.

It's Hard suffers from all the same problems as *Face Dances*, only more so: there's no unity between lyrics and melody, the music is irritatingly bitty and light, the songs are ineffective, Roger isn't suited to sing them, John Entwistle's tracks again sound like the work of a different act altogether and Glyn Johns' production couldn't repeat previously inspired results.

Pete was no longer interested in The Who. His own solo albums were superior affairs and it's really no surprise that the best track on *It's Hard*, 'Eminence Front', is more of a Townshend solo effort than a band recording. The rest are a grab bag of second-raters, often bland and confusing or both, always lacking power and nothing less than a pale shadow of the songs he wrote a decade before.

Released to coincide with what was billed as The Who's 1982 'farewell' tour of America, which included two nights at Shea Stadium in New York, it reached Number 11 in the UK and 8 in the US.

ATHENA

A PROMISING rumble that echoes the old Who opens the album in encouraging fashion, especially as Roger and Pete exchange vocals and Pete slows down the tempo to sing a middle-eight. A stabbing brass section dodges in and out of the chorus and Kenney Jones lets rip with a few drum rolls, but 'Athena', whoever she may be, is out of reach.

IT'S YOUR TURN
(Entwistle)

IN WHAT was now becoming a habit, Roger sang an Entwistle song, and in a curious way John's songs seemed more appropriate to Daltrey's style than many of those that Pete was submitting. Here there's a dense backing track but the song strides along at a solid rock tempo, featuring Andy Fairweather-

Low on rhythm guitar, which suggests Pete wasn't present when it was recorded. The song is about ageing, and passing on the baton to the next generation of rock and rollers.

COOKS COUNTY

WITH AN odd time signature, convoluted backing and undecipherable lyrics that seem to be about human suffering, this song never settles down and is quite forgettable. Particularly unsuitable for Roger.

IT'S HARD

EVEN ROGER, eternally The Who's up-front flag waver and source of energy, seems to have lost his enthusiasm here. The vocals drag and, despite an upbeat chorus, so does the song. As the title implies, this is a song about life being tough, and it must have been so in the studio when they recorded this cliché ridden effort. Played on stage with Roger on guitar, the opening lines were originally from another Townshend original, 'Popular' (released on his 1983 demo collection *Scoop*).

DANGEROUS
(Entwistle)

SYNTHESIZERS and John's twangy bass dominate another dense

and rather lumpy anonymous rocker, which was also performed on the '82 farewell tour.

EMINENCE FRONT

THE BEST song on the album and the least Who-like of them all, 'Eminence Front' has a tense, springy tempo underlined by synthesizer patterns and a nagging little riff that carries the slight but catchy melody. Some nice, loose guitar lines thread their way in and out but with no block chords, no Roger (he played guitar when Pete sang this one on stage), and no outstanding bass line, it's as if this was an entirely different band from the one that played the last track. This, of course, is probably what Pete wanted for his song about putting on a façade to hide behind.

I'VE KNOWN NO WAR

SYNTHESIZER dominates Pete's musings on the end of World War II and his birth immediately after Germany surrendered. Roger again seems unsuited to sing this but the monotonous pace doesn't help. Melodically uninteresting, the song just doesn't go anywhere at all.

ONE LIFE'S ENOUGH

A VERY short experimental piece with Roger singing light opera style over piano and synthesizer. Mannered and taken at a strict tempo, Roger must have wondered whether Pete was off his rocker when he offered material like this to The Who.

ONE AT A TIME
(Entwistle)

FOR ONLY the second time in The Who's career, John gets three songs on an album, but all three come at the same tempo. This one opens with a slightly off key brass figure, includes more synthesizers and features John on vocals singing about the woman troubles that have plagued him ever since his bank balance went into the black.

WHY DID I FALL FOR THAT?

THERE'S a typical Who chord change midway through the solo in this otherwise anonymous piece, but where's the guitar? Quality control was clearly out to lunch as Pete dredged up songs as uninspired as this...

A MAN IS A MAN

AND THIS. Roger and Pete swap vocal lines on another slight, forgettable ballad which drags along until alternate lines speed up during the chorus. Eminently forgettable.

CRY IF YOU WANT

THE FINAL studio song The Who released as a group for almost ten years is an unmelodious piece about past indiscretions with a difficult tempo that features military drum patters to build up the drama. Just as forgettable as so many other songs on this weak, insipid album.

Bonus Tracks on Remastered CD

IT'S HARD

EMINENCE FRONT

DANGEROUS

CRY IF YOU WANT

ALL FOUR tracks were recorded live at Maple Leaf Gardens, Toronto, December 1982.

LATER LIVE RELEASES

TO ELABORATE, THE LATER TAG REFERS LARGELY TO CONCERT RELEASES postdating 1983 when Pete Townshend announced his departure from The Who, encompassing the 1989 25th Anniversary tour, the 1996/97 Quadrophenia shows, and UK/US concerts from 1999 to John Entwistle's death in 2002. Additional archive concert releases featuring Keith Moon are detailed (see also the *Live At Leeds* and *Who's Next* entries). Unfortunately, there is a paucity of quality live material from this later period and not nearly enough material from The Who's first decade. For continuity's sake these releases are presented in the order in which they were recorded, not in the order they were released.

The Monterey International Pop Festival

US: Rhino CD R2 70596, released October 1992, reissue R2 72825;
UK Castle ROK CD 102, 1997

THIS FOUR-CD BOX SET INCLUDES THE WHO'S ENTIRE 25-MINUTE performance from June 18, 1967. On a smaller scale than Woodstock, Monterey played a pivotal role in building The Who's credibility across America. It is also the basis for various legends about the band and Jimi Hendrix jockeying for prime position in the final evening's running order as neither wanted to follow the other. Even if true, the interminable jamming of The Grateful Dead that intervened was probably sufficient in negating any disadvantage of going first. More germane is the fact that the band went on stage using borrowed equipment and their performance suffered as a result.

The Who's set comprised 'Substitute', 'Summertime Blues', 'Pictures Of Lily', 'A Quick One (While He's Away)', 'Happy Jack' and 'My Generation'.

Live At The
Isle Of Wight Festival
1970

UK: CD Castle Communications EDF CD 326, 1996;
US: CD Columbia C2X 65084, 1996

FOR YEARS RUMOURS SUGGESTED THAT FILM AND AUDIO OF THE WHO'S performance at the third Isle of Wight Festival in August 1970 not only existed but also confirmed that the *Leeds* show was more than a "one-off". In the mid-Nineties, original director Murray Lerner dug out his film and the original 8-track tapes (along with some of the other festival acts) were found in Pete Townshend's tape archive. Negotiations finally resulted in the release of a double CD and a VHS video in 1996, with a triple vinyl and DVD release following in 2001.

Generally, the rumours regarding the quality of the show proved true. The Who sounded brash and aggressive and provided an emotional excitement in their performance while at the top of their game. Unsurprisingly, in view of its proximity to *Live At Leeds*, the two shows are quite similar, even if the *Isle Of Wight* comes off as slightly second best.

DISC ONE: 'Heaven And Hell', 'I Can't Explain', 'Young Man Blues', 'I Don't Even Know Myself', 'Water', 'Overture', 'It's A Boy', '1921', 'Amazing Journey', 'Sparks', 'Eyesight To The Blind (The Hawker)', 'Christmas'.

DISC TWO: 'The Acid Queen', 'Pinball Wizard', 'Do You Think It's Alright?', 'Fiddle About', 'Tommy Can You Hear Me?', 'There's A Doctor', 'Go To The Mirror!', 'Smash The Mirror', 'Miracle Cure', 'I'm Free', 'Tommy's Holiday Camp', 'We're Not Gonna Take It', 'Summertime Blues', 'Shakin' All Over'/'Twist And Shout', 'Substitute', 'My Generation', 'Naked Eye', 'Magic Bus'.

Who's Last

Original UK issue: LP MCA WHO 1, released December 1984;
CD: MCA MCAD WHO1, MCA MCLD 19005
US: MCA MCA2-8018, released November 1984; CD: MCA MCAD2-8018

IT'S A CRYING SHAME THAT **T**HE **W**HO WAITED UNTIL **1984** TO RELEASE A full-blown double LP designed to represent an entire concert. By this time they'd given up touring completely and this came out almost as an afterthought, although at one time there were plans, regrettably abandoned, to include retrospective material from the early Seventies.

This release is a reasonably accurate reflection of the way the band sounded on the 1982 US tour, and by any standards apart from their own, they didn't sound bad at all. They'd become what Roger and John always wanted: a streamlined, professional, major league rock attraction, capable of selling out vast arenas to fans who wanted to hear a diet of classic songs from The Who's splendid back catalogue. Roger and John (and Kenney Jones) were happy to oblige; Pete wasn't but he went along anyway, knowing that he had nothing left creatively to offer The Who.

Most of the young crowds who came to see The Who in 1982 hadn't seen them before and knew nothing of the glorious spark that illuminated them in days gone by. The fans sang along to 'See Me, Feel Me', punched the air to 'Won't Get Fooled Again' and played air guitars to 'My Generation', and then went home happy, well satisfied with what The Who had given them. The Who got well paid (at last!), so why should anyone complain?

Well, for starters it was a shoddy state of affairs that any live material from this era – recorded when the band was coasting – should find its way on to the market legitimately, while there was very little live material available – *Leeds* excepted – from the era when The Who genuinely reigned as the world's greatest live rock band. Secondly, *Who's Last* was heard by younger critics of the band – not to mention younger potential fans with perceptive ears – who inevitably turned around and quite rightly questioned if there was anything special that set The Who above and apart from other bands (as one critic put it, "wished they'd died before they got old."). Thirdly, most of these tracks were taken from the Toronto show that had been released on video the previous year (see *The Who Rocks America* below), so hardcore fans already had this material. Older fans with treasured memories just shook their heads in resignation. Even the packaging – a dodgy 'Union Jack burning' cover in the UK and dull black and gold effort in the US – was rank. What had happened to quality control? Why would The Who willingly allow their reputation to be trashed in this way? Didn't they care any more? Who knows (or cared)?

Keith Moon would have rolled over in his grave if he'd heard it. It's to be hoped he didn't.

TRACKS: 'My Generation', 'I Can't Explain', 'Substitute', 'Behind Blue Eyes', 'Baba O'Riley', 'Boris The Spider', 'Who Are You', 'Pinball Wizard', 'See Me, Feel Me', 'Love, Reign O'er Me', 'Long Live Rock', 'Live Rock (Reprise)', 'Won't Get Fooled Again', 'Dr Jimmy', 'Magic Bus', 'Summertime Blues', 'Twist And Shout'.

Join Together

Original UK issue: Virgin VDT 102, CD: Virgin VSCD 102, reissue Virgin CDVDT 102, March 1990,
US: MCA MCA3-19501, CD: MCA MCAD2-19501, March 1990

IN THE US *JOIN TOGETHER* WAS A BOXED DOUBLE ALBUM PACKAGE OF THE **1989** reunion tour, designed as a memento from that project and little else. It features Pete, Roger and John augmented by many other musicians – *two* drummers (which Keith Moon had always sounded like), keyboards, an extra guitarist, brass section and choir – recorded live in America. The more cynical critics have called it the 'Las Vegas Who', and once again older fans cringed at what they heard. It didn't sell and hit the remaindered bins within months of release.

But at least this time there was no heartless attempt at trying to sound like what the Who had once been. Everybody accepted that this was an exercise in nostalgia and the prevailing mood on tour was mercifully free of angst as a result. In a heart-warming speech at Wembley Arena, Pete Townshend admitted that the band on stage was no longer The Who and that they'd done this tour principally for the money. It was difficult to argue with the fact that The Who had served rock well over the years and deserved finally to reap the kind of rewards that many lesser bands had earned years before.

For the record, the first half of the double album features a selection of *Tommy* songs, followed by Who hits in the second and, for the first time on record, a Pete solo song – 'Rough Boys' – essayed by the band. There's also a live rendition of 'I Can See For Miles' which the four man Who found difficult to perform live originally because it required two guitars. Another first was Pete playing acoustic guitar on stage (ostensibly due to hearing problems) and some of his rhythmic chord work, especially on the early *Tommy* tunes, is first rate, evidence indeed that while his song-writing talents might have waned over the years, his ability as a guitarist had, if anything, improved.

DISC ONE: 'Overture', '1921', 'Amazing Journey', 'Sparks', 'The Hawker (Eyesight To The Blind)', 'Christmas', 'Cousin Kevin', 'The Acid Queen', 'Pinball Wizard', 'Do You Think It's Alright?', 'Fiddle About', 'There's A Doctor', 'Go To The Mirror', 'Smash The Mirror', 'Tommy Can You Hear Me?', 'I'm Free', 'Miracle Cure', 'Sally Simpson', 'Sensation', 'Tommy's Holiday Camp', 'We're Not Gonna Take It'.

DISC TWO: 'Eminence Front', 'Face The Face', 'Dig', 'I Can See For Miles', 'A Little Is Enough', '5:15', 'Love, Reign O'er Me', 'Trick Of The Light', 'Rough Boys', 'Join Together', 'You Better You Bet', 'Behind Blue Eyes', 'Won't Get Fooled Again'.

The Blues To The Bush
1999

UK: No release | US: CD Musicmaker.com 2931496, April 2000

A SELECTION FROM THE WHO'S LOW-KEY 'COMEBACK' PERFORMANCES (in October 1999 at Chicago's House Of Blues, and December 1999 at London's Shepherd's Bush Empire) as a sensibly stripped-down five-piece featuring Roger, Pete, John, Rabbit Bundrick (keyboards), and Zak Starkey (drums).

DISC ONE: 'I Can't Explain', Substitute', 'Anyway Anyhow Anywhere', 'Pinball Wizard', 'My Wife', 'Baba O'Riley', 'Pure And Easy', 'You Better You Bet', 'I'm A Boy', 'Getting In Tune', 'The Real Me'.

DISC TWO: 'Behind Blue Eyes', 'Magic Bus', 'Boris The Spider', 'After The Fire', 'Who Are You', '5:15', 'Won't Get Fooled Again', 'The Kids Are Alright', 'My Generation'.

Live At The
Royal Albert Hall

UK: CD SPV 093-74882, released June 2003,
SACD Hybrid SPV 096-74880*, December 2003
US: Release used EU product, same information as above.

THIS IS A SURPRISINGLY GOOD PERFORMANCE, DESPITE OR BECAUSE OF THE various guest stars involved. The majority was recorded at a charity performance at the Royal Albert Hall on November 27, 2000, most of which had previously been available on DVD (see below). The four tracks on the Bonus Disc emanate from a Royal Albert Hall show on February 8, 2002, which unfortunately marked the final on-stage appearance of John Entwistle.

DISC ONE: 'I Can't Explain', 'Anyway Anyhow Anywhere', 'Pinball Wizard', 'Relay', 'My Wife', 'The Kids Are Alright', 'Mary Anne With The Shaky Hand', 'Bargain', 'Magic Bus', 'Who Are You', 'Baba O'Riley (with Nigel Kennedy).

DISC TWO: 'Drowned', 'Heart To Hang Onto', 'So Sad About Us' (PT and Paul Weller), 'I'm One' (with Eddie Vedder), 'Getting In Tune (with Eddie Vedder)',' 'Behind Blue Eyes' (with Bryan Adams), 'You Better You Bet', 'The Real Me', '5:15', 'Won't Get Fooled Again' (with Noel Gallagher), 'Substitute' (with Kelly Jones), 'Let's See Action' (with Eddie Vedder), 'My Generation'/'See Me, Feel Me'/'Listening To You' (with Eddie Vedder & Bryan Adams).

BONUS DISC: 'I'm Free', 'I Don't Even Know Myself', 'Summertime Blues', 'Young Man Blues'.

* = The SACD hybrid's second disc stops after 'Won't Get Fooled Again' and places the remaining tracks, including the bonus tracks on Disc Three.

2002 US TOUR - OFFICIAL BOOTLEGS

FOLLOWING JOHN ENTWISTLE'S DEATH IN JUNE 2002 ON THE EVE OF A US TOUR, Roger and Pete elected to carry on by drafting in talented session player, Pino Palladino. In anticipation that bootlegs would flourish, plans were announced to make available official soundboard recordings via The Who's official website. (Pearl Jam had just done the same thing successfully for recent European and US tours.)

The performances are uniformly professional, but recording quality varies. These releases are interesting for those wanting to hear how The Who sounds today. Zak Starkey is an excellent addition to the millennium Who and proves the natural successor (if there could be such a thing) to Keith Moon. However, no one show stands out as an indispensable release. So therefore the onus is on the buyer – collect them all or take a chance with a representational one (or two).

The Who Live Mountain View, CA
3 July 2002

DISC ONE: 'I Can't Explain', 'Substitute', 'Anyway Anyhow Anywhere', 'Who Are You', 'Another Tricky Day', 'Relay', 'Bargain', 'Baba O'Riley', 'Eminence Front', 'Sea And Sand', '5:15', 'Love Reign O'er Me'.

DISC TWO: 'Behind Blue Eyes', 'You Better You Bet', 'The Kids Are Alright', 'My Generation', 'Won't Get Fooled Again', 'Pinball Wizard', 'Amazing Journey', 'Sparks', 'See Me, Feel Me', 'Listening To You'.

The Who Live Marysville, CA
4 July 2002

DISC ONE: 'I Can't Explain', 'Substitute', 'Anyway Anyhow Anywhere', 'Who Are You', 'Another Tricky Day', 'Relay', 'Bargain', 'Baba O'Riley', 'Eminence Front', 'Sea And Sand', '5:15', 'Love Reign O'er Me'.

DISC TWO: 'Behind Blue Eyes', 'You Better You Bet', 'The Kids Are Alright', 'My Generation', 'Won't Get Fooled Again', 'Pinball Wizard', 'Amazing Journey', 'Sparks', 'See Me, Feel Me', 'Listening To You'.

The Who Live George, WA
6 July 2002

DISC ONE: 'I Can't Explain', 'Substitute', 'Anyway Anyhow Anywhere', 'Who Are You', 'Another Tricky Day', 'Relay', 'Bargain', 'Baba O'Riley', 'Eminence Front', 'Sea And Sand', '5:15', 'Love Reign O'er Me'.

DISC TWO: 'Behind Blue Eyes', 'You Better You Bet', 'The Kids Are Alright', 'My Generation', 'Won't Get Fooled Again', 'Pinball Wizard', 'Amazing Journey', 'Sparks', 'See Me, Feel Me', 'Listening To You'.

The Who Live Mansfield, MA
26 July 2002

DISC ONE: 'I Can't Explain', 'Substitute', 'Anyway Anyhow Anywhere', 'Who Are You', 'Another Tricky Day', 'Relay', 'I Can See For Miles', 'Baba O'Riley', 'Eminence Front', 'Sea And Sand', '5:15', 'Love Reign O'er Me'.

DISC TWO: 'Behind Blue Eyes', 'You Better You Bet', 'The Kids Are Alright', 'My Generation', 'Won't Get Fooled Again', 'Pinball Wizard', 'Amazing Journey', 'Sparks', 'See Me, Feel Me', 'Listening To You'.

The Who Live Camden, NJ
27 July 2002

DISC ONE: 'I Can't Explain', 'Substitute', 'Anyway Anyhow Anywhere', 'Who Are You', 'Another Tricky Day', 'Relay', 'Bargain', 'Baba O'Riley', 'Eminence Front', 'Sea And Sand', '5:15', 'Love Reign O'er Me'.

DISC TWO: 'Behind Blue Eyes', 'You Better You Bet', 'The Kids Are Alright', 'My Generation', 'Won't Get Fooled Again', 'Pinball Wizard', 'Amazing Journey', 'Sparks', 'See Me, Feel Me', 'Listening To You'.

The Who Live Hershey, PA
29 July 2002

DISC ONE: 'I Can't Explain', 'Substitute', 'Anyway Anyhow Anywhere', 'Who Are You', 'Another Tricky Day', 'Relay', 'Bargain', 'Baba O'Riley', 'Sea And Sand', '5:15', 'Love Reign O'er Me'.

DISC TWO: 'Eminence Front', 'Behind Blue Eyes', 'You Better You Bet', 'The Kids Are Alright', 'My Generation', 'Won't Get Fooled Again', 'Pinball Wizard', 'Amazing Journey', 'Sparks', 'See Me, Feel Me', 'Listening To You'.

The Who Live New York, NY
31 July 2002

DISC ONE: 'I Can't Explain', 'Substitute', 'Anyway Anyhow Anywhere', 'Who Are You', 'Another Tricky Day', 'Relay', 'Bargain', 'Baba O'Riley', 'Sea And Sand', '5:15', 'Love Reign O'er Me'.

DISC TWO: 'Eminence Front', 'Behind Blue Eyes', 'You Better You Bet', 'The Kids Are Alright', 'My Generation', 'Won't Get Fooled Again', 'Pinball Wizard', 'Amazing Journey', 'Sparks', 'See Me, Feel Me', 'Listening To You'.

The Who Live New York, NY
3 August 2002

DISC ONE: 'I Can't Explain', 'Substitute', 'Anyway Anyhow Anywhere', 'Who Are You', 'Another Tricky Day', 'Relay', 'Bargain', 'Baba O'Riley', 'Sea And Sand', '5:15', 'Love Reign O'er Me'.

DISC TWO: 'Eminence Front', 'Behind Blue Eyes', 'You Better You Bet', 'The Kids Are Alright', 'My Generation', 'Won't Get Fooled Again', 'Pinball Wizard', 'Amazing Journey', 'Sparks', 'See Me, Feel Me', 'Listening To You'.

The Who Live New York, NY
4 August 2002

DISC ONE: 'I Can't Explain' 'Substitute', 'Anyway Anyhow Anywhere', 'Who Are You', 'Another Tricky Day', 'Relay', 'Bargain', 'Baba O'Riley', 'Sea And Sand', '5:15', 'Love Reign O'er Me'.

DISC TWO: 'Eminence Front', 'Behind Blue Eyes', 'You Better You Bet', 'The Kids Are Alright', 'My Generation', 'Won't Get Fooled Again', 'Pinball Wizard', 'Amazing Journey', 'Sparks', 'See Me, Feel Me', 'Listening To You'.

The Who Live Detroit, MI
23 August 2002

DISC ONE: 'I Can't Explain' , 'Substitute', 'Anyway Anyhow Anywhere', 'Who Are You', 'Another Tricky Day', 'Relay', 'Bargain', 'Baba O'Riley', 'Sea And Sand', '5:15', 'Love Reign O'er Me'.

DISC TWO: 'Eminence Front', 'Behind Blue Eyes', 'You Better You Bet', 'The Kids Are Alright', 'My Generation', 'Won't Get Fooled Again', 'Pinball Wizard', 'Amazing Journey', 'Sparks', 'See Me, Feel Me', 'Listening To You'.

The Who Live Tinley Park, IL
24 August 2002

DISC ONE: 'I Can't Explain' , 'Substitute', 'Anyway Anyhow Anywhere', 'Who Are You', 'Another Tricky Day', 'Relay', 'Bargain', 'Baba O'Riley', 'Sea And Sand', '5:15', 'Love Reign O'er Me'.

DISC TWO: 'Love Reign O'er Me', 'Eminence Front', 'Behind Blue Eyes', 'You Better You Bet', 'The Kids Are Alright', 'My Generation', 'Won't Get Fooled Again', 'Pinball Wizard', 'Amazing Journey', 'Sparks', 'See Me, Feel Me', 'Listening To You'.

The Who Live Noblesville, IN
25 August 2002

DISC ONE: 'I Can't Explain' , 'Substitute', 'Anyway Anyhow Anywhere', 'Who Are You', 'Another Tricky Day', 'Relay', 'Bargain', 'Baba O'Riley', 'Sea And Sand', '5:15', 'Love Reign O'er Me'.

DISC TWO: 'Eminence Front', 'Behind Blue Eyes', 'You Better You Bet', 'The Kids Are Alright', 'My Generation', 'Won't Get Fooled Again', 'Pinball Wizard', 'Amazing Journey', 'Sparks', 'See Me, Feel Me', 'Listening To You'.

The Who Live Grand Rapids, MI
27 August 2002

DISC ONE: 'I Can't Explain', 'Substitute', 'Anyway Anyhow Anywhere', 'Who Are You', 'Another Tricky Day', 'Relay', 'Bargain', 'Baba O'Riley', 'Sea And Sand', '5:15', 'Love Reign O'er Me'.

DISC TWO: 'Eminence Front', 'Behind Blue Eyes', 'You Better You Bet', 'The Kids Are Alright', 'My Generation', 'Won't Get Fooled Again', 'Pinball Wizard', 'Amazing Journey', 'Sparks', 'See Me, Feel Me', 'Listening To You'.

The Who Live Columbus, OH
28 August 2002

DISC ONE: 'I Can't Explain', 'Substitute', 'Anyway Anyhow Anywhere', 'Who Are You', 'Another Tricky Day', 'Bargain', 'Baba O'Riley', 'Sea And Sand', '5:15', 'Love Reign O'er Me', 'Eminence Front'.

DISC TWO: 'Behind Blue Eyes', 'You Better You Bet', 'The Kids Are Alright', 'My Generation', 'Won't Get Fooled Again', 'Pinball Wizard', 'Amazing Journey', 'Sparks', 'See Me, Feel Me', 'Listening To You'.

The Who Live Holmdel, NJ
30 August 2002

DISC ONE: 'I Can't Explain', 'Substitute', 'Anyway Anyhow Anywhere', 'Who Are You', 'Another Tricky Day', 'Relay', 'Bargain', 'Baba O'Riley', 'I'm One', 'Sea And Sand', '5:15', 'Love Reign O'er Me'.

DISC TWO: 'Behind Blue Eyes', 'You Better You Bet', 'The Kids Are Alright', 'My Generation', 'Won't Get Fooled Again', 'Pinball Wizard', 'Amazing Journey', 'Sparks', 'See Me, Feel Me', 'Listening To You'.

The Who Live Wantaugh, NY
31 August 2002

DISC ONE: 'I Can't Explain', 'Substitute', 'Anyway Anyhow Anywhere', 'Who Are You', 'Another Tricky Day', 'Relay', 'Bargain', 'Baba O'Riley', 'I'm One', 'Sea And Sand', '5:15', 'Love Reign O'er Me'.

DISC TWO: 'Behind Blue Eyes', 'You Better You Bet', 'The Kids Are Alright', 'My Generation', 'Won't Get Fooled Again', 'Pinball Wizard', 'Amazing Journey', 'Sparks', 'See Me, Feel Me', 'Listening To You'.

The Who Live Las Vegas, NV
14 September 2002

DISC ONE: 'I Can't Explain', 'Substitute', 'Anyway Anyhow Anywhere', 'Who Are You', 'Another Tricky Day', 'Relay', 'Bargain', 'Baba O'Riley', 'I'm One', 'Sea And Sand', '5:15', 'Love Reign O'er Me'.

DISC TWO: 'Behind Blue Eyes', 'You Better You Bet', 'The Kids Are Alright', 'My Generation', 'Won't Get Fooled Again', 'Pinball Wizard', 'Amazing Journey', 'Sparks', 'See Me, Feel Me', 'Listening To You'.

The Who Live Irvine, CA
15 September 2002

DISC ONE: 'I Can't Explain', 'Substitute', 'Anyway Anyhow Anywhere', 'Who Are You', 'Another Tricky Day', 'Relay', 'Bargain', 'Baba O'Riley', 'I'm One', 'Sea And Sand', '5:15', 'Love Reign O'er Me'.

DISC TWO: 'Behind Blue Eyes', 'You Better You Bet', 'The Kids Are Alright', 'My Generation', 'Won't Get Fooled Again', 'Pinball Wizard', 'Amazing Journey', 'Sparks', 'See Me, Feel Me', 'Listening To You'.

The Who Live Los Angeles, CA
17 September 2002

DISC ONE: 'I Can't Explain', 'Substitute', 'Anyway Anyhow Anywhere', 'Who Are You', 'Another Tricky Day', 'Relay', 'Bargain', 'Baba O'Riley', 'I'm One', 'Sea And Sand', '5:15'.

DISC TWO: 'Love Reign O'er Me', 'Behind Blue Eyes', 'You Better You Bet', 'The Kids Are Alright', 'My Generation', 'Won't Get Fooled Again', 'Pinball Wizard', 'Amazing Journey', 'Sparks', 'See Me, Feel Me', 'Listening To You'.

The Who Live Denver, CO
19 September 2002

DISC ONE: 'I Can't Explain', 'Substitute', 'Anyway Anyhow Anywhere', 'Who Are You', 'Another Tricky Day', 'Relay', 'Bargain', 'Baba O'Riley', 'Sea And Sand', '5:15', 'Love Reign O'er Me'.

DISC TWO: 'Eminence Front', 'Behind Blue Eyes', 'You Better You Bet', 'The Kids Are Alright', 'My Generation', 'Won't Get Fooled Again', 'Pinball Wizard', 'Amazing Journey', 'Sparks', 'See Me, Feel Me', 'Listening To You'.

The Who Live Dallas, TX
21 September 2002

DISC ONE: 'I Can't Explain', 'Substitute', 'Anyway Anyhow Anywhere', 'Who Are You', 'Another Tricky Day', 'Relay', 'Bargain', 'Baba O'Riley', 'Sea And Sand', '5:15', 'Love Reign O'er Me'.

DISC TWO: 'Eminence Front', 'Behind Blue Eyes', 'You Better You Bet', 'The Kids Are Alright', 'My Generation', 'Won't Get Fooled Again', 'Pinball Wizard', 'Amazing Journey', 'Sparks', 'See Me, Feel Me', 'Listening To You'.

The Who Live Chicago, IL
23 September 2002

DISC ONE: 'I Can't Explain', 'Substitute', 'Anyway Anyhow Anywhere', 'Who Are You', 'I Don't Even Know Myself', 'Baba O'Riley', 'Sea And Sand', '5:15', 'Love Reign O'er Me', 'Eminence Front'.

DISC TWO: 'Behind Blue Eyes', 'The Kids Are Alright', 'My Generation', 'Won't Get Fooled Again', 'Pinball Wizard', 'Amazing Journey', 'Sparks', 'See Me, Feel Me', 'Listening To You'.

The Who Live St. Paul, MN
24 September 2002

DISC ONE: 'I Can't Explain', 'Substitute', 'Anyway Anyhow Anywhere', 'Who Are You', 'Another Tricky Day', 'Relay', 'Bargain', 'Baba O'Riley', 'Sea And Sand', '5:15', 'Love Reign O'er Me'.

DISC TWO: 'Eminence Front', 'Behind Blue Eyes', 'You Better You Bet', 'The Kids Are Alright', 'My Generation', 'Won't Get Fooled Again', 'Pinball Wizard', 'Amazing Journey', 'Sparks', 'See Me, Feel Me', 'Listening To You'.

The Who Live Mansfield, MA
27 September 2002

DISC ONE: 'I Can't Explain', 'Substitute', 'Anyway Anyhow Anywhere', 'Who Are You', 'Another Tricky Day', 'Relay', 'Bargain', 'Baba O'Riley', 'Sea And Sand', '5:15', 'Love Reign O'er Me'.

DISC TWO: 'Eminence Front', 'Behind Blue Eyes', 'You Better You Bet', 'The Kids Are Alright', 'My Generation', 'Won't Get Fooled Again', 'Pinball Wizard', 'Amazing Journey', 'Sparks', 'See Me, Feel Me', 'Listening To You'.

The Who Live Toronto, ON
28 September 2002

DISC ONE: 'I Can't Explain', 'Substitute', 'Anyway Anyhow Anywhere', 'Who Are You', 'Another Tricky Day', 'Relay', 'Bargain', 'Baba O'Riley', 'Sea And Sand', '5:15', 'Love Reign O'er Me'.

DISC TWO: 'Eminence Front', 'Behind Blue Eyes', 'You Better You Bet', 'The Kids Are Alright', 'My Generation', 'Won't Get Fooled Again', 'Pinball Wizard', 'Amazing Journey', 'Sparks', 'See Me, Feel Me', 'Listening To You'.

COMPILATIONS

THIS SECTION DEALS WITH **UK** AND **US** SELECTED COMPILATIONS, INCLUDING full track listings, with a focus on CD releases.

Despite Keith Moon's remark that The Who would never be compiled into collections of previously issued material, Track Records repackaged and reissued numerous Who songs and albums in their budget 'Backtrack' series during the Seventies. Polydor in the UK and MCA in the US have subsequently followed with more compilations as "The hits just keep on coming – again and again!"

As a result, few back catalogues have been pillaged as rapaciously as The Who's. In the UK alone, Who fans have possibly bought eight greatest hits albums/CDs – three of them doubles – which offer similar track listings. Add slightly different US hits albums put out by MCA, not to mention Who compilations from elsewhere in the world, and the figure runs well into the dozens. Many are badly mastered and a Spanish hits LP even had a stage shot of Track stablemates, Golden Earring, on the cover that purported to be The Who. So much for quality control.

The first Who compilation album was *Magic Bus – The Who On Tour* [Decca 5064 mono, Decca 75064 stereo; US CD: MCA MCAD-31333]. Decca (US) released it in September 1968 to capitalise on interest in The Who generated by their extensive touring that year. The Who had quickly realised that their best chance of success was as a live band, but with this release, Decca unwittingly did its corporate best to scupper those chances. For starters, the title gave a false impression that it was a live album; even worse, several tracks were badly mastered, and the entire concept – sleeve design and packaging – was just plain awful, outdated, and naïve. It could have seriously affected The Who's US reputation were it not so blatantly obvious to anyone who knew anything about group that they had absolutely nothing to do with it. The band were furious. The full *Magic Bus* track listing was 'Disguises', 'Run Run Run', 'Dr. Jekyll And Mr. Hyde', 'I Can't Reach You', 'Our Love Was (Is)', 'Call Me Lightning', 'Magic Bus', 'Someone's Coming', 'Doctor, Doctor', 'Bucket T' and 'Pictures Of Lily'.

The first UK compilation, *Direct Hits* [Track 612 006 mono; 613 006 stereo; unreleased on CD] came out in October 1968 and gathered together a rather motley collection of early singles, B-sides, and album tracks. It was by no means comprehensive as far as singles were concerned, lacking any Shel Talmy productions which makes it inadequate as a retrospective of The Who's career to that point. The full *Direct Hits* track listing was 'Bucket T', 'I'm A Boy', 'Pictures Of Lily', 'Doctor, Doctor', 'I Can See For Miles', 'Substitute', 'Happy Jack', 'The Last Time', 'In The City', 'Call Me Lightning', 'Mary Anne With The Shaky Hand' [acoustic version] and 'Dogs'.

One of the least likely promotional stunts to which The Who lent their name in 1972 was the sponsorship of a rally car. Quite why this necessitated Pete and Keith being photographed sipping champagne with underwear-clad models is uncertain, but neither seems to have been unduly unhappy about it.

October 3, 1973: Pete on stage at the BBC TV Centre in London, filming '5.15' from *Quadrophenia* for *Top Of The Pops*. As the song finished Pete smashed his Gretsch guitar (a gift from Joe Walsh) and Keith destroyed his kit but this was edited out of the show when it was broadcast the following night. It was later reported that The Who had been 'banned for life' from TOTP as a result, but they did appear again, eight years later. Keith, however, was definitely banned for life from the BBC Club bar following a dispute with a commissionaire.
Inset: *Quadrophenia* (1973) and *Odds And Sods* (1974).

Caution: Craftsman at work. John on stage in October, 1975.

The Who By Number (1975), featuring John's join-up-the-dots artwork.

Who Are You (1978), the last Who album to feature Keith on drums.

The soundtrack to *The Kids Are Alright* (1979) featuring a shot of The Who taken in New York in April 1968 at the foot of Grant's Tomb, with the group draped in a giant Union Jack flag, exhausted from having been thrown out of a hotel the previous night.

The soundtrack to the *Quadrophenia* movie (1979) featuring Phil Daniels as Jimmy, in the Brighton alley where he and Leslie Ash consummated their brief relationship.

Pete on stage at the Hammersmith Odeon, on December 28, 1979.

Faces Dances (1981) and *It's Hard* (1982).

Roger and Pete on stage at Live Aid, Wembley Stadium, July 13, 1985.

Who's Missing (1985) and Two's Missing (1987) were US only compilations that offered previously material and sleeve notes from Pete and John respectively.

Pete on stage during The Who's 25th Anniversary tour, October 1989. During this period Pete was playing acoustic guitars on stage due to problems with tinnitus.

Roger and John in 1995.

Thirty Years Of Maximum R&B
(1994), the Who's 4-CD box set.

My Generation: The Very Best Of...
(1996), one of too many
compilation albums that have
appeared over the years;
The Who's *BBC Sessions* (2000)

John, Roger and Pete in New York City in 2000, announcing a US tour.

THE ULTIMATE COLLECTION

The Ultimate Collection (2002).

Pete on stage, London, 2000.

The Who, Then And Now (2004), which contained two new Who songs, their first new material for 22 years.

Meaty Beaty
Big & Bouncy

UK: Original issue Track 1406 006; October 1971; unreleased on CD.
US: Decca DL 79184, November 1971, CD: MCAD 37001

MEATY BEATY BIG & BOUNCY WAS RELEASED IN BOTH THE UK AND US, and unlike earlier compilations thankfully included Talmy's essential early productions (much to Kit Lambert's chagrin). With an attractive gatefold sleeve and a specially shot cover photo by Roger's cousin Graham Hughes, it easily remains the Who retrospective by which all others are measured. The running order was again chronologically awry, but it went a long way towards introducing new American fans to The Who's early UK triumphs. In an article that Pete wrote for Rolling Stone, he described *Meaty Beaty* as the best ever Who album and he was probably right.

The full track listing is 'I Can't Explain', 'The Kids Are Alright', 'Happy Jack', 'I Can See For Miles', 'Pictures Of Lily', 'My Generation', 'The Seeker', 'Anyway Anyhow Anywhere', 'Pinball Wizard', 'A Legal Matter', 'Boris The Spider', 'Magic Bus', 'Substitute' and 'I'm A Boy'.

I CAN'T EXPLAIN

SEE *My Generation* Deluxe Edition.

THE KIDS ARE ALRIGHT

SEE *My Generation*. The original UK *Meaty Beaty* illogically overlooked the full-length version of this track and, like the US album and CD, used the edited American version instead.

WHEN Cliff Townshend, Pete's father, played saxophone in the RAF dance band The Squadronaires, the Isle of Man was a regular gig and Pete was dragged along, hence the Isle of Man reference in this great mid-Sixties Who single.

At the end of the song Pete can be heard yelling 'I saw yer' to Moon who was trying to edge in on the vocals, now forbidden territory in view of his inability to sing on key. In a nod to nostalgia, audiences often yell 'I saw yer' at the end of the song when The Who perform it live.

'Happy Jack' reached Number 3 in the UK charts in December 1966, and the became The Who's first US hit, reaching Number 24.

See also *Live At Leeds* bonus tracks.

blue period."

'Lily' reached Number 4 in the UK charts and was the first single by The Who to be released on Track Records, the label formed by their co-managers Kit Lambert and Chris Stamp.

See also *Live At Leeds* bonus tracks.

I CAN SEE FOR MILES

SEE *The Who Sell Out*.

MY GENERATION

SEE *My Generation*.

PICTURES OF LILY

NEVER ONE to be coy in his choice of subject material, here's Pete's early observations on masturbation, written from the point of view of the young lad whose dad sympathises with his son's raging hormones and offers relief in the form of soft-core pictures. 'Lily' was quite daring for its time (1967), and even today might likely generate a ban from sensitive radio stations and a headline in the tabloid press on a quiet news day, Page Three notwithstanding. Between the verses John steps forth on the French horn, which he played in a Boys' Brigade band in his early teens.

John: "It's all about wanking... Townshend going through his sexual traumas – something that he did quite often. I suppose you could say this record represents our smutty period, or to be more refined, our

THE SEEKER

THE WHO were never a heavy metal band, but this track – with its 'heavy' repeated riff and rather lumbering rhythm track – comes close. However the introspective, yearning and evidently heart-felt lyrics are anything but heavy metal, and describe Pete's 'desperate' search for a meaning to his life, whether it be through his peers (references to Dylan, and The Beatles) or drugs (Timothy Leary). It was a poor choice for a single immediately following *Tommy* and reached only Number 19 in the UK and 44 in the US. 'The Seeker' has subsequently been used in movies – most notably *American Beauty* (2000).

ANYWAY ANYHOW ANYWHERE
(Townshend/Daltrey)

THE WHO'S second single slipped between two tall stools, 'Explain' and 'Generation', but again allowed Roger the opportunity to spit out boastful lyrics about invincibility which, for the first and almost the last time on a Who song, he helped write himself. What is most notable about 'Anyway' is the feedback noise guitar solo – in this instance coupled with Nicky Hopkins' rolling piano – that would be repeated to greater effect on 'Generation'. Here producer Shel Talmy was trying to bring The Who's stage act to the studio, trying to record The Who as they sounded live.

Pete: "I wrote the first verse and Roger helped with the rest. I was inspired by listening to Charlie Parker, feeling that this was a free spirit, and whatever he'd done with drugs and booze and everything else, that his playing released him and freed his spirit, and I wanted us to be like that, and I wanted to write a song about that, a spiritual song."

'Anyway' made No 10 in the UK and, more importantly, was chosen as the theme tune for *Ready, Steady, Go!*, the groundbreaking weekly rock TV show on which The Who would be featured many times.

See *My Generation* Deluxe Edition for what apparently was the original take intended for the UK/US single which ended up on an early French EP.

PINBALL WIZARD

SEE *Tommy*.

A LEGAL MATTER

SEE *My Generation*.

BORIS THE SPIDER

SEE *A Quick One*.

MAGIC BUS

THE ORIGINAL album had an unexpected surprise by including a longer unedited and slightly different studio version of The Who's Bo Diddley influenced single, which had been released in 1968. The CD purports to include the longer version as well, but actually includes the single. Supposedly, initial pressings of the Canadian *Meaty Beaty* CD carry the longer version.

SUBSTITUTE

MANY FANS' choice as the best Who single of all time, 'Substitute' is a timeless comment on image tampering and illusion, set to one hell of a tricky little riff, all driven along by an omnipotent ringing open D string and – for the

-first time – that big fat acoustic sound Pete first heard on 'Three Steps To Heaven' by Eddie Cochran. Now a bona fide pop classic, 'Substitute' endured throughout The Who's live career, and was played at virtually every concert they ever performed from then on.

Pete has stated that he felt The Who were a substitute for The Rolling Stones and this is what inspired the song. He also liked the use of the word in Smokey Robinson & The Miracles' classic 'The Tracks Of My Tears'. Pete had heard 'Where Is My Girl?' by Robb Storme & The Whispers, a little known 1965 Columbia (UK) single, during a *Melody Maker* interview. That song very conveniently provided the melody during the verses for 'Substitute'. In America the controversial line, "I look all white but my dad was black" was changed to "I try going forward but my feet walk back", which reflects America's over-reaction to potentially sensitive comments on racial matters at this time.

Aside from its musical values – and the fact that it was the first record that Pete Townshend had ever produced himself – 'Substitute' has an interesting history as a single. It was released three times in the UK in March 1966, with a different B-side each time (although two of the B-sides were the same song with a different title). The third version contained on its B-side an instrumental entitled 'Waltz For A Pig' by 'The Who Orchestra' which was actually the Graham Bond Organisation. This was the most public manifestation of the Shel Talmy (a.k.a. the pig!) problem.

'Substitute' reached Number 5 in the UK charts but flopped in the US where it became the only Who single to be issued through Atlantic Records, on their Atco subsidiary.

See also *Live At Leeds* bonus tracks.

I'M A BOY

I'M A BOY' was originally written as part of a longer project called *Quads*, a Townshend tale set in the future when parents could choose the sex of their children. The family in the story requested four girls but got three girls and a boy, and this single is the boy's lament at the error. With lyrics quite unlike any other pop song of the period, it tips a hat to The Beach Boys with its high harmonies, but the great counterpoint between guitar and drums is 100% Who.

The original single recording was produced by Kit Lambert at IBC Studios on August 1, 1966, and released as a single just over three weeks later. Unfortunately it stalled at Number 2 in the UK singles charts while the late Jim Reeves occupied the top spot with 'Distant Drums'. This is a second, longer version, apparently intended for the *A Quick One* album, featuring John on French horn.

IN A SEEMINGLY ENDLESS PROGRAMME OF REISSUES, OFTEN TIMED TO APPEAR when the band went out on tour, many other major retrospectives of The Who have been released by either MCA or Polydor. Key US/UK releases are listed below.

The Story Of The Who

Original UK issue: LP Polydor 2683 069, September 1976.
US: No release

SIDE ONE: 'Magic Bus', 'Substitute', 'Boris The Spider', 'Run Run Run', 'I'm A Boy', 'Heat Wave', 'My Generation' (edit from *Live At Leeds*)

SIDE TWO: 'Pictures Of Lily', 'Happy Jack', 'The Seeker', 'I Can See For Miles', 'Bargain', 'Squeeze Box'.

SIDE THREE: 'Amazing Journey', 'Acid Queen', 'Do You Think It's Alright?', 'Fiddle About', 'Pinball Wizard', 'I'm Free', 'Tommy's Holiday Camp', 'We're Not Gonna Take It', 'Summertime Blues' (edit from *Live At Leeds*),

SIDE FOUR: 'Baba O'Riley', 'Behind Blue Eyes', 'Slip Kid', 'Won't Get Fooled Again'.

Phases

Original UK release: Polydor 2675 216, May 1981
US: No release

ALTHOUGH TECHNICALLY A UK RELEASE, ALL COPIES OF THIS 9-LP BOX SET project were manufactured in West Germany. The quality of the vinyl was excellent overall, which continues to makes this a decent vinyl overview of the basic Who catalogue. The set included *My Generation, A Quick One, The Who Sell Out, Tommy, Live At Leeds, Who's Next, Quadrophenia, The Who By Numbers,* and *Who Are You.*

Hooligans

UK: No release | US: LP MCA MCA2-12001, September 1981;
CD MCA MCAD-12001

DISC ONE: 'I Can't Explain', 'I Can See For Miles', 'Pinball Wizard', 'Let's See Action', 'Summertime Blues' (from *Live At Leeds*)', 'The Relay', 'Baba O'Riley', 'Behind Blue Eyes', 'Bargain', 'The Song Is Over'.

DISC TWO: 'Join Together', 'Squeeze Box', 'Slip Kid', 'The Real Me', '5.15', 'Drowned', 'Had Enough', 'Sister Disco', 'Who Are You'.

Who's Greatest Hits

UK: No release | US: LP MCA MCA-5408, released April 1983, CD: MCA MCAD-1496

TRACKS: 'Substitute', 'The Seeker', 'Magic Bus', 'My Generation', 'Pinball Wizard', 'Happy Jack', 'Won't Get Fooled Again' (edited), 'My Wife', 'Squeeze Box', 'The Relay', 'Love, Reign O'er Me', 'Who Are You'.

Rarities Vol. 1 1966-69

UK: LP Polydor SPELP 9, CD Polydor 847 670-2, August 1983
US: No release

IN THE EARLY EIGHTIES, POLYDOR COMPILED TWO ALBUMS OF OTHERWISE unavailable Who tracks – mostly obscure B-sides – on *Rarities Vol 1 and Vol 2*. Polydor subsequently combined both volumes into one budget-priced CD. In a similar move, MCA issued two albums entitled *Who's Missing* and *Two's Missing*, both of which were somewhat more imaginative in that they contained then previously unreleased tracks. The ongoing CD upgrade program should eventually make these releases redundant.

TRACKS: 'Circles' (aka 'Instant Party'), 'Disguises', 'Batman', 'Bucket T', 'Barbara Ann', 'In The City', 'I've Been Away', 'Doctor Doctor', 'The Last Time', 'Under My Thumb', 'Someone's Coming', 'Mary Anne With the Shaky Hand(s)', 'Dogs', 'Call; Me Lightning', Dr Jekyl And Mr. Hyde'.

Tracks not dealt with above as are follows:

THE LAST TIME
(Jagger/Richards)

WHEN Mick Jagger and Keith Richards were up on drug charges in June 1967, The Who decided to offer their support by recording this track and 'Under My Thumb' as a single and to bung it out *tout de suite*. Apparently it was their intention to record one Stones track a month until the Glimmer Twins were released but fortunately for all concerned, the errant Stones were sprung before The Who got around to recording any others. A good job too... The Who's effort is workmanlike but despite an upward key change towards the end, lacks both the attack and the menace of the Stones' version. Pete played bass because John was away on his honeymoon, aboard the QEII.

MARY ANNE WITH THE SHAKY HAND(S)

THIS IS A completely different recording from that used on the original *The Who Sell Out* LP. This 'electric' version features Roger's voice through a tremolo effect to give that s-h-a-k-y sound, and there's an understated organ solo from Al Kooper. Lacking the bounce of the acoustic version, it was used as the US B-side of the 'I Can See For Miles' single. The initial LP pressing mistakenly used the album version.

See *The Who Sell Out* and *Odds And Sods* CDs for summary on the various versions available.

DOGS

A CONTENDER for the strangest single The Who ever released, 'Dogs' is clearly influenced by the Cockney rock style of The Small Faces on 'Lazy Sunday', or even Ray Davies' eccentric Englishness that resulted in so many great Kinks songs. It's a sympathetic, quite complex song, about the British working class male's love of greyhound racing and beer, almost comical but with just the right amount of Who-like influences and performance to suggest that Pete really meant it. The closing vocal 'armonies are quite luvverly. Released in June 1968, it stalled at No. 25.

CALL ME LIGHTNING

'CALL ME Lightning' was one of the first songs written by Pete Townshend, around the same time as 'I Can't Explain', and was even suggested for their first single. Its mildly funky R&B feel is emphasised by chanted surf backing vocals, with Roger emoting as best he could on lyrics that no-one bar Pete understood. John gets a twangy bass solo, which he never regarded highly.

Pete: "It tries to be a slightly surly Jan & Dean kind of song to satisfy Keith and John's then interest in surf music, which I thought was going to be a real problem. Being a trumped up Mod band was bad enough for us to handle, but trying to be a trumped-up Mod band playing R&B music with surf overtones was almost impossible... this song was trying to be all things to all men."

'Lightning' was the UK B-side of 'Dogs' but in the US a version with a different mix was a 1968 single in its own right and reached Number 40.

DR. JEKYLL AND MR. HYDE
(Entwistle)

JOHN'S attempt to translate Hammer horror into his music succeeds admirably, with a scary opening, menacing bass line and spooky French horn. Indeed, John's bass carries the melody and, at the climax, he manages both a wicked scream and a rather macabre growl. A novelty item, it appeared as the B-side to 'Call Me Lightning' in the US and on the B-side of the UK 'Magic Bus' single in 1968.

Rarities Vol. 2

LP Polydor SPELP 10, CD Polydor 847 670-2, 1983 | US: No release

JOIN TOGETHER

OPENING with Roger on Jew's harp and harmonica, or possibly Pete on synthesizer reproducing the sound of a Jew's harp, 'Join Together' was a key song in 'Lifehouse' which expresses Pete's ultimate fantasy of band and audience becoming one. Although – like its companion piece 'Let's See Action' – its rhythms bear little relation to the power chord style normally projected by The Who, the band play it quite superbly, jostling together with effortless syncopation. 'Join Together' was issued as a single in June 1972 and it reached Number 9 in the charts.

I DON'T EVEN KNOW MYSELF

SEE *Who's Next* bonus tracks.

HEAVEN AND HELL
(Entwistle)

JOHN WAS never happy with this studio version of 'Heaven And Hell' which rocked along as well as anything Pete was writing at the time. It was often used as a warm-up number to open Who sets between 1968 and 1970, allowing Pete an opportunity to flex his fingers on the solo and Keith to get his arms into gear. First released as the B-side of the 'Summertime Blues' single in 1970.

WHEN I WAS A BOY
(Entwistle)

A TASTEFULLY arranged brass introduction sets the mood for John's nostalgic song about age and disillusionment. More sincere than is usual for Entwistle, 'When I Was A Boy' was definitely one of his better Who songs, though the production is weak. Released as the B-side of 'Let's See Action' single in 1971.

LET'S SEE ACTION

A CALL TO arms and another uncharacteristic single from the early Seventies, 'Let's See Action' has an almost folksy feel, although a trilling piano from Nicky Hopkins carries the slight, rather laborious melody and the song is overlong. The contrast between Roger's determined vocal and Pete's more introspective middle-eight intrusion is both assured and reassuring. It wasn't a hit (briefly it reached Number 16) but The Who hadn't lost their way: Pete was just experimenting in order to avoid stagnation.

RELAY

W AH-WAH guitar, or 'treated synthesizer guitar', opens a full-tilt rocker about the need to exchange ideas and information or at least pass them on to the next generation. With a ringing acoustic guitar in one channel and the wah-wah in the other, not to mention John's exemplary bass playing high up the fretboard, there's a wealth of good ideas, both musical and lyrical, here; also, a nice allegory about passing on the baton in a relay race. Far too weighty as a single, it reached Number 21 in early 1973.

WASPMAN
(Moon)

T HREE minutes of pure lunacy allegedly originated by Keith during a long and boring flight across America when he adopted the guise of a wasp and ran around the plane making buzzing noises with a groupie's bra wrapped around his face.

Relocated to the recording studio Keith continues to buzz while the band play a truly monotonous three-chord riff. It would be generous to describe the result as filler material. On other instrumentals credited to Keith in the past he'd made a point of doing something special on the drums, but alas, not this time. The B-side of the 'Relay' single, released November 1972.

HERE FOR MORE
(Daltrey)

ROGER'S second solo composing credit in The Who's catalogue – the first was 'See My Way' back in 1966 – is a fairly lightweight country and western style song without The Who's normal attack which possibly means that Keith was absent from the session. Despite its authentic country licks and lap-steel guitar, The Who were never in danger of becoming The Eagles (for which one can be thankful). Released as the B-side of 'The Seeker' in March 1970.

WATER

SEE *Who's Next* bonus tracks.

BABY DON'T YOU DO IT
(Holland/Dozier/Holland)

RECORDED live at the San Francisco Civic on December 13, 1971, this is a fierce work-out on the Tamla song recorded by Marvin Gaye, highlighted by Keith's energetic drumming, Roger's strident vocals and The Who's unique ability to turn soul into furious rock at the drop of a hat. With the band on the same form as they were the night they recorded *Live At Leeds*, this track presents The Who at their live best, playing off one another as no other band could, with each outstanding individually as well. There's some lovely bass work, and Pete's buzz-saw guitar solo towards the end is terrific. During a furious 'head for home' climax Pete, John and Keith play their hearts out with Roger hollering to be heard above the din. Then, just to stress the point, there's a false ending and the band rev up yet again.

The Who often played this song live during 1971 but abandoned it because the songs from *Who's Next* offered them a wider choice of quality material. It appeared as the B-side of the 'Join Together' single.

See comments for *Who's Next* CD tracks discussing a studio version.

The Who Collection

UK: LP Polydor/CBS/Impression IMDP 4, October 1985;
CD: IMCD4/1 and IMCD4/2, reissue Polydor SMD 570. | US: No release

DISC ONE: 'I Can't Explain', 'Anyway Anyhow Anywhere', 'My Generation', 'Substitute', 'A Legal Matter', 'The Kids Are Alright', 'I'm A Boy', 'Happy Jack', 'Boris The Spider', 'Pictures Of Lily', 'I Can See For Miles', 'Won't Get Fooled Again', 'The Seeker', 'Let's See Action', 'Join Together', 'Relay', 'Love Reign O'er Me', 'Squeeze Box'.

DISC TWO: 'Who Are You', 'Long Live Rock', '5.15', 'You Better You Bet', 'Magic Bus', Summertime Blues', 'Shakin' All Over', 'Pinball Wizard', 'The Acid Queen', 'I'm Free', 'We're Not Gonna Take It', 'Baba O'Riley', 'Behind Blue Eyes', 'Bargain'.

The Singles

Original UK issue: LP POLYDOR WHOD 17, released November 1984;
CD: Polydor 815 965 5-2

TRACKS: 'Substitute', 'I'm A Boy', 'Happy Jack', 'Pictures Of Lily', 'I Can See For Miles', 'Magic Bus', 'Pinball Wizard', 'My Generation', 'Summertime Blues', 'Won't Get Fooled Again', 'Let's See Action', 'Join Together', 'Squeeze Box', 'Who Are You', 'You Better You Bet'.

Who's Missing

US LP: MCA MCA-5641, November 1985; CD MCA MCAD-31221

TRACKS: 'Leaving Here', 'Lubie', 'Shout And Shimmy', 'Anytime You Want Me', 'Barbara Ann', 'I'm A Boy' (alternate take), 'Mary Anne With The Shaky Hands' [sic] (electric version), 'Heaven And Hell', 'Here For More', 'I Don't Even Know Myself', 'When I Was A Boy', 'Bargain' (live).

Tracks not dealt with above are as follows:

LEAVING HERE
(Holland/Dozier/Holland)

THIS VERSION is the same Shel Talmy produced take that later appeared on the *My Generation* Deluxe Edition (see entry), but features a different Daltrey vocal track on this version. See *Odds & Sods* CD tracks for an alternate version.

BARGAIN

THE WHO live at their very best... taken from the show recorded at San Francisco on December 13, 1971 (see 'Baby Don't You Do It' on *Rarities Vol.2*) when they were at their height as the live band. Incorporates a false ending, thumping coda and blitzkrieg climax. Also included in edited form on *30 Years Of Maximum R&B* (see below).

Two's Missing

US LP: MCA MCA-5712, April 1987, CD: MCA MCAD-31222

TRACKS: 'Bald Headed Woman', 'Under My Thumb', 'My Wife' (live, San Francisco, 1971), 'I'm A Man', 'Dogs', 'Dogs Part II', 'Circles', 'The Last Time', 'Water', 'Daddy Rolling Stone', 'Heat Wave' (original version), 'Going Down (live)', 'Motoring', 'Waspman'.

Tracks not dealt with above are as follows:

GOING DOWN
(Freddie King)

Recorded live in San Francisco, December 13, 1971, this is a slow but heavy blues jam on a Freddie King song with negligible vocals, typical of how The Who might stretch the climax of any number of songs in their catalogue, depending on their mood on the night. Pete's guitar dominates, but John and Keith provide him with a superb platform.

Who's Better Who's Best

UK: Polydor 835 389-1/2, March 1988;
US LP: MCA MCA2-8031, November 1988, CD: MCA MCAD-8031

ALTHOUGH A FAMILIAR TRACK LISTING, *WHO'S BETTER WHO'S BEST* IS STILL worth seeking out for the interesting insights in the sleeve notes provided by Richard Barnes, a close friend of Pete Townshend.

TRACKS: 'My Generation', 'Anyway Anyhow Anywhere', 'The Kids Are Alright', 'Substitute', 'I'm A Boy', 'Happy Jack', 'Pictures Of Lily', 'I Can See For Miles', 'Who Are You', 'Won't Get Fooled Again', 'Magic Bus', 'I Can't Explain', 'Pinball Wizard', 'I'm Free', 'See Me, Feel Me', 'Squeeze Box', 'Join Together', 'You Better You Bet' *(CD bonus track)*, 'Baba O'Riley'.

My Generation - The Very Best Of The Who

UK: CD Polydor 533 150-2, 1996
US: CD MCA MCAD-11462, released August 1996

WHY WAS *MEATY BEATY BIG & BOUNCY* OVERLOOKED FROM THE CD REISSUE programme? As an album it stands up as a classic but it would have been rather sparse as an upgraded CD, especially considering the CD format's technological ability to handle 80 minutes of music. Expanding *Meaty Beaty*, on the other hand, would turn it into something the original LP was not. One solution was a new anthology – a full CD with remixed and remastered tracks – in chronological order. Using a horrible cover design didn't help, but that's a whole other story. *Meaty Beaty Big & Bouncy* is still the album to own and somehow less is more.

TRACKS: 'I Can't Explain', 'Anyway Anyhow Anywhere', 'My Generation', 'Substitute', 'I'm A Boy', 'Boris The Spider', 'Happy Jack', 'Pictures Of Lily', 'I Can See For Miles', 'Magic Bus', 'Pinball Wizard', 'The Seeker', 'Baba O'Riley', 'Won't Get Fooled Again (full length version)', 'Let's See Action', '5.15', 'Join Together', 'Squeeze Box', 'Who Are You (single edit version)', 'You Better You Bet' (full length version).

The Best Of The Who

UK: No release | US: CD MCA MCAD-11951, April 1999

MCA ISSUED THIS AS PART OF ITS '20TH CENTURY MASTERS: THE MILLENNIUM Collection'. Viewed as an acknowledgement of The Who's contribution to the last century's musical landscape, this otherwise ordinary collection takes on some minor rationale for release.

TRACKS: 'My Generation', 'Happy Jack', 'I Can See For Miles', 'Magic Bus', 'Pinball Wizard', 'Squeeze Box', 'Behind Blues Eyes', 'Who Are You', 'Join Together', 'Won't Get Fooled Again'.

BBC Sessions

UK: LP Polydor 547 72701, CD: Polydor 547 727-2, February 2000
US CD: MCA 088 111 960-2, February 2000

THANKS TO THE BBC'S STRANGLEHOLD OVER UK RADIO 'NEEDLE TIME' FOR records during the Sixties, Musicians Union regulations often required "live" recordings for airplay. While an annoyance for many groups and artists of the time, these historical artifacts (the ones that survived the BBC's archive purges) are now a collector's delight and provide an insight into The Who's true musical abilities when forced to duplicate their recorded sound. In some instances both band and management would often try to get out of this situation by submitting remixed studio tapes over which Roger would sing a new vocal take.

UK TRACK LISTING: 'My Generation' (Radio 1 Jingle), 'Anyway Anyhow Anywhere', 'Good Lovin' (Clark/Resnick), 'Just You And Me, Darling' (Brown), 'Leaving Here', 'My Generation', 'The Good's Gone', 'La La La Lies', 'Substitute', 'Man With Money', 'Dancing In The Street' (Stevenson/Gaye/Hunter), 'Disguises', 'I'm A Boy', 'Run Run Run', 'Boris The Spider', 'Happy Jack', 'See My Way' (Cochran), 'Pictures Of Lily', 'A Quick One (While He's Away)', 'Substitute', 'The Seeker', 'I'm Free', 'Shakin' All Over'/'Spoonful' (Dixon), 'Relay', 'Long Live Rock', 'Boris The Spider' (Radio 1 Jingle).

Due to publishing complications the US track listing eliminated 'Man With Money' and edited out the few lines from 'Spoonful' contained in 'Shakin' All Over'. However initial copies of the CD came packaged with...

Live At The BBC

UK: No release | US CD: Point Entertainment PNT9091, February 2000

A BONUS DISC of BBC versions, available only in the US through the Best Buy chain, accompanied the initial release of *BBC Sessions*.

TRACKS: Townshend Talks *Tommy*, 'Pinball Wizard', 'See Me, Feel Me', 'I Don't Even Know Myself', 'I Can See For Miles', 'Heaven And Hell', 'The Seeker', 'Summertime Blues'.

The Who - The Ultimate Collection

UK: CD Polydor 065 234-2 and 065 300-2, October 2002
US: CD MCA 088 112 877-2, June 2002

ANOTHER EFFORT TO EXPAND ON *MEATY BEAT BIG & BOUNCY*, **THIS IS CERTAINLY** a comprehensive overview of the Who's UK and US singles but over-looks at least two, 'Relay' and 'Slip Kid,' not to mention others such as 'La La La Lies', 'Dogs', and 'See Me, Feel Me'. Originally intended only for release in the US to coincide with The Who's tour there, Polydor in the UK decided to issue their own version in a different (and elaborate) gatefold package with a bonus CD Rom containing tracks from the BBC's film of The Who at Charlton in 1974. Considering the other greatest hits packages still available, particularly in the US, it's hard to understand the rationale for this release. At least there are two different sleeves and a few extra tracks on the UK version for the collector.

DISC ONE: 'I Can't Explain', 'Anyway Anyhow Anywhere', 'My Generation', 'The Kids Are Alright', 'A Legal Matter', 'Substitute', 'I'm A Boy', 'Boris The Spider', 'Happy Jack', 'Pictures Of Lily', 'I Can See For Miles', 'Call Me Lightning', 'Magic Bus', 'Pinball Wizard', 'I'm Free', 'See Me, Feel Me', 'The Seeker', 'Summertime Blues' (live), 'My Wife', 'Baba O'Riley', 'Bargain',

(Disc Two of the US version begins here) 'Behind Blue Eyes', 'Won't Get Fooled Again'

DISC TWO: 'Let's See Action', 'Pure And Easy', 'Join Together', 'Long Live Rock', 'The Real Me', '5:15', 'Love Reign O'er Me', 'Squeeze Box', 'Who Are You', 'Had Enough' (not included on US version), 'Sister Disco', 'You Better You Bet', 'Don't Let Go The Coat', 'The Quiet One', 'Another Tricky Day', 'Athena' (the last four tracks not included on US version), 'Eminence Front'.

BONUS DISC: 'Substitute (US Single Version)', 'I'm A Boy' (album version), 'Happy Jack' (acoustic version – contrary to sleeve notes previously released as a bonus track on *A Quick One* CD), 'Magic Bus' (remixed single version), 'Baba O'Riley' (Live Charlton 74), 'Substitute' (Live Charlton 74)

(Tracks 5-6 not included on US version)

Then And Now 1964 - 2004

UK: No release | US: CD, Geffen Records, release due March 2004

IN CONJUNCTION WITH ROGER AND PETE'S EFFORTS TO PRODUCE THE FIRST NEW Who studio tracks in over 20 years, we get yet another anthology. This one is released only in the States, while the UK gets a box set of "singles". See below.

DISC ONE: 'I Can't Explain', 'My Generation, 'The Kids Are Alright, 'Substitute', 'I'm A Boy', 'Happy Jack', 'I Can See For Miles', 'Magic Bus', 'Pinball Wizard', 'See Me Feel Me'.

DISC TWO: ' 'Summertime Blues' (live), 'Behind Blue Eyes, 'Won't Get Fooled Again', '5:15', 'Love, Reign O'er Me', 'Squeeze Box, 'Who Are You', 'You Better You Bet', 'Real Good Looking Boy', 'Old Red Wine'.

The First Singles Box

UK: CD, Polydor 986 633 8, released April 2004 | US: No release

IN CONTRAST TO THE NEARLY SIMULTANEOUS US RELEASE OF *THEN AND NOW* 1964-2004 (see above), the UK got a box set of 12 CD singles, with copies of rare pictures sleeves and record labels. Generally, the correct single mixes are used, with the exception of 'In The City', 'Pinball Wizard', and 'Dogs Part Two'. Overall, a much more interesting package than *Then And Now*, with promises of a second set in the future.

CD-1: 'I Can't Explain' (Original mono version), 'Bald Headed Woman'

CD-2: 'My Generation' (Original mono version), 'Shout And Shimmy'

CD-3: 'Substitute' (Single Version), 'Circles' (Revised/Second mono version)

CD-4: 'I'm A Boy' (Mono Version), 'In The City' ("Stereo" version)

CD-5: 'Happy Jack' (Single version), 'I've Been Away'

CD-6: 'Pictures Of Lily', 'Doctor Doctor'

CD-7: 'I Can See For Miles', 'Someone's Coming'

CD-8: 'Pinball Wizard' (Original album version), 2. 'Dogs Part Two' (2003 stereo version)

CD-9: 'Won't Get Fooled Again', 'Don't Know Myself' (sic)

CD-10: '5:15' (Single version), 'Water' (Studio version)

CD-11: 'Who Are You' (Single version), 'Had Enough'

CD-12: 'Real Good Looking Boy', 'Old Red Wine'

30 Years Of
Maximum R&B

UK: Polydor 521 751-2, July 1994; US: MCA MCAD4-11020, 1994

IN JULY 1994, TO MARK THE FORTIETH ANNIVERSARY OF THE WHO'S FIRST RECORD release (as The High Numbers) Polydor/MCA released a four CD box set (also a four cassette version in the US) containing all their best known work, several rarities and a number of previously unreleased recordings. Many of the tracks were punctuated by soundbites – the group talking amongst themselves in the studio, Pete making announcements from the stage or Keith telling jokes – and the package included a sumptuous 72-page full colour booklet with essays by Pete Townshend, Who PR man Keith Altham and Dave Marsh. It also included a comprehensive Who chronology, a discography by Who archivist Ed Hanel and credits that gave an abundance of recording details not previously available.

Most of the 79 tracks, bar those recorded with Shel Talmy, were remastered and/or remixed and the sound quality is uniformly excellent. This is especially noticeable on the three songs by The Who as The High Numbers and the tracks produced by Kit Lambert in the Sixties. Even without access to the master tapes the Talmy recordings were tidied up as best as possible by co-producer Jon Astley, who originally co-produced the *Who Are You* album with Glyn Johns.

The package was extremely well received by critics. *Q* magazine in the UK gave it a maximum five stars rating and described it as the best box set ever produced by any artist; similarly, *Rolling Stone* magazine in the US gave it a maximum five stars too. The most common criticism was the omission of the original 'Substitute' in favour of the live version recorded at Leeds; other critics felt that the post-Keith Moon era was under represented, though the compilers were all of the opinion that the real Who existed only while Keith was alive, and that his drumming was such an essential part of The Who's music that scant attention should be paid to the post-Moon era. Only six tracks out of 79 don't feature Keith.

In a short essay at the end of the booklet the compilers explain their reasons for including certain tracks and for excluding others. The full track listing is as follows:

CD 1: 'Pete dialogue*†', 'I'm The Face', 'Here 'Tis*', 'Zoot Suit', 'Leaving Here', 'I Can't Explain', 'Anyway Anyhow Anywhere', 'Daddy Rolling Stone', 'My Generation', 'The Kids Are Alright', 'The Ox', 'A Legal Matter', 'Pete dialogue*', 'Substitute†', 'I'm A Boy', 'Disguises', 'Happy Jack Jingle*', 'Happy Jack', 'Boris

The Spider', 'So Sad About Us', 'A Quick One†', 'Pictures Of Lily', 'Early Morning Cold Taxi*', 'Coke 2*', 'The Last Time', 'I Can't Reach You; Girl's Eyes*', 'Bag O'Nails*', 'Call Me Lightning'

CD 2: 'Rotosound Strings', 'I Can See For Miles', 'Mary Anne With The Shaky Hand', 'Armenia City In The Sky', 'Tattoo', 'Our Love Was', 'Rael 1', 'Rael 2*', 'Track Records* – Premier Drums', 'Sunrise', 'Jaguar*', 'Melancholia*', 'Fortune Teller*', 'Magic Bus', 'Little Billy', 'Russell Harty dialogue*†', 'Dogs', 'Overture', 'Acid Queen', 'Abbie Hoffman Incident*†', 'Underture†', 'Pinball Wizard', 'I'm Free', 'See Me, Feel Me*†', 'Heaven And Hell', 'Pete dialogue*', 'Young Man Blues†', 'Summertime Blues†'

CD 3: 'Shakin' All Over†', 'Baba O'Riley', 'Bargain†', 'Pure And Easy', 'The Song Is Over', 'Studio dialogue*†', 'Behind Blue Eyes', 'Won't Get Fooled Again', 'The Seeker (edit)', 'Bony Moronie†', 'Let's See Action', 'Join Together', 'Relay', 'The Real Me*', '5:15 (single mix)', 'Bell Boy', 'Love Reign O'er Me'

CD 4: ' Long Live Rock', 'Life With The Moons*', 'Naked Eye*†', 'University Challenge*', 'Slip Kid', 'Poetry Cornered*', 'Dreaming From The Waist*†', 'Blue Red And Grey', 'Life With The Moons 2*', 'Squeeze Box', 'My Wife*†', 'Who Are You', 'Music Must Change', 'Sister Disco', 'Guitar And Pen', 'You Better You Bet', 'Eminence Front', 'Twist And Shout*†', 'I'm A Man*†', 'Pete dialogue*†', 'Saturday Night's Alright For Fighting'.

* denotes recording previously unreleased or unavailable in this version.
† denotes live recording.

The following tracks that appear on *Maximum R&B* have not previously been analysed:

HERE 'TIS
(Ellis McDaniel)

A PREVIOUSLY unreleased record-ing of The High Numbers play-ing a song by Bo Diddley that was a fixture in their 1964 live act. It was also covered the same year by con-temporaries The Yardbirds at a much faster pace on their *Five Live Yardbirds* album. Nice harmony singing and guitar fills, with the beat carried by maracas. Simple but enjoyable.

FORTUNE TELLER
(Neville)

B ENNY Spellman's hit 'Fortune Teller', also covered by The Rolling Stones, was a staple of The Who's live act between 1968 and 1970. This lively studio version, recorded in 1968, remained unre-leased until the box set was issued.

ABBIE HOFFMAN INCIDENT

JUST AFTER The Who had performed 'Pinball Wizard' during their rendering of *Tommy* at Woodstock on August 17, 1969, the late yippie politico Abbie Hoffman walked on stage and began a harangue through Pete's mike on behalf of imprisoned radical comrade John Sinclair. Pete yelled a few imprecations then unceremoniously clubbed him off stage with his guitar. Although Pete later regretted his hasty action, the incident is part of Who folklore and is preserved for posterity here.

SEE ME, FEEL ME

A FORCEFUL live version of the climax to *Tommy* recorded live at Leeds University during the February 14 1970 show that produced The Who's *Live At Leeds* album. The 'See Me, Feel Me' introduction is actually taken from the studio recording, apart from the final refrain, because Roger sang this section off key on the night.

THE REAL ME

A PREVIOUSLY unreleased reworking of the *Quadrophenia* song taken from the audition for Kenney Jones at Ramport Studio, London, in January 1979.

LIFE WITH THE MOONS 1&2, UNIVERSITY CHALLENGE, POETRY CORNERED

FOUR SET piece comedy items from Keith Moon's BBC radio series from 1973.

BONY MORONIE
(Williams)

A RAGGED but entertaining blast through the Larry Williams rock 'n'roll standard recorded live at London's Young Vic on April 26, 1971. Pete's guitar lacks precision and Keith sometimes isn't quite sure where to go next, but John's sturdy bass holds things together and Roger, ever at home on an old rocker, gives a truly great vocal performance. The Who as a bar band; definitely worth two quid on the door.

MY WIFE
(Entwistle)

A BLISTERING version of John's 'My Wife', recorded live at Swansea Football Ground on June 12, 1976.

TWIST AND SHOUT
(Medley/Burns)

THE WHO frequently ended their 1982 shows with a full tilt version of 'Twist And Shout' from The Beatles' *Please Please Me* album which in turn was a re-reading of

The Isley Brothers' version. John Entwistle takes lead vocals as he did in the early days of The Detours when the song was part of the group's repertoire. Fun but certainly not essential.

I'M A MAN
(McDaniel)

A LONG reading of the Bo Diddley swaggerer, first recorded by The Who back in 1965 on their début album, and taken from the 1989 reunion tour featuring a cast of thousands. Roger over-eggs the pudding a bit with his appeals for crowd participation, but there's no denying the enthusiasm of the audience and the band – even at this late stage in their career. This track did not appear on *Join Together*, the official souvenir of the 1989 tour.

SATURDAY NIGHT'S ALRIGHT FOR FIGHTING
(John, Taupin)

T HE WHO recorded Elton John's 'Saturday Night's Alright For Fighting' (originally on his million-selling 1973 album *Goodbye Yellow Brick Road*) for a 1991 tribute album of Elton John/Bernie Taupin compositions entitled *Two Rooms* which also featured Joe Cocker, Kate Bush, Sting, George Michael and many others. With Jon Astley on drums, Pete, Roger and John make the song their own, which segues neatly half way through into Pete's vocal on 'Border Song', thus bringing out the contrast between Roger and Pete's voices as in days of old.

And Finally...

A RECORDING OF *TOMMY* BY THE LONDON SYMPHONY ORCHESTRA AND Chamber Choir (UK: ODE SP 88 001; US: ODE SP 99 001) was released worldwide in November/December 1972. Lou Reizner produced the project, featuring Pete Townshend, Roger Daltrey and John Entwistle among an all star cast that also included Sandy Denny, Steve Winwood, Ringo Starr and Rod Stewart. It was subsequently released on CD in 1994: (UK) Castle Communications ESM CD 404 and (US) Ode ODECD 1972.

Pete, working with Des McAnuff, also developed a successful May 1993 Broadway version of *Tommy*, which he then sent on the road around the US and the London's West End. The score is available in its entirety on a CD double disc: (US) BMG 09026-61874-2 and in an edited single disc version: (US) 09026-62522-2.

Additional live recordings by The Who appear on the following albums:

WOODSTOCK (UK Atlantic 2663 001, released 1970; reissue K60001; US Atlantic 82636, CD Atlantic SD 500-2): 'We're Not Gonna Take It'.

CONCERTS FOR THE PEOPLE OF KAMPUCHIA (UK Atlantic K60153, released March 1981; US Atlantic SD-2 7005): 'Baba O'Riley', 'Sister Disco', 'Behind Blue Eyes', 'See Me, Feel Me'.

THE ROLLING STONES ROCK AND ROLL CIRCUS (ABKCO 1268-2, released October 1996): 'A Quick One (While He's Away)'.

THE CONCERT FOR NEW YORK CITY (US: Columbia C2K 86270, released November 2001): 'Who Are You', 'Baba O'Riley' and 'Won't Get Fooled Again'.

TWO SONGS CREDITED TO THE WHO (WITH SIMON PHILLIPS ON DRUMS) CAN BE found on Pete Townshend's *Iron Man* LP (Virgin CDV 2592, released March 1989):

FIRE
(Brown, Crane, Ker, Finesilver)

THE WHO seem quite at home on their radical re-write of one-time Track labelmate Arthur Brown's 1968 chart topper, though there's little similarity between The Who and Brown. Lacking the terror-filled passion of Arthur Brown's version, The Who use a synthesizer backdrop and build up to an almost 'Day In The Life' style crescendo.

DIG

FEATURED live during the 1989 reunion tour because Pete was ostensibly promoting his *Iron Man* album at the time, 'Dig' rolls along at a relaxed country pace, and fea-

tures a deep voiced Roger and jangly-style guitar solo. The repeated refrain "The old ones have seen two wars" at the end of each verse has a nice poignancy.

Just for the record, the only officially released song *credited* to The Who that is not available on any CD album in either the UK or the US at the time of writing is their cover of Martha & The Vandellas' 'Dancing In The Street', recorded live at the Philadelphia Spectrum on December 13, 1979, which appeared as an extra track on a single re-issue of 'Won't Get Fooled Again' in June 1988.

Who2 - 2004

IN APRIL 2004 THE WHO RELEASED THEIR FIRST PROPER RECORDINGS SINCE 1982 (discounting 'Fire' and 'Saturday Night's Alright For Fighting' on Pete Townshend's *Iron Man* [1989] and the Elton John/Bernie Taupin tribute album *Two Rooms* [1991] respectively), a single 'Real Good Looking Boy'/'Old Red Wine' recorded as part of a project originally mooted as a complete new Who album of songs to be jointly written by Townshend and Daltrey. In the US these songs appeared on a compilation album entitled *Then And Now 1964-2004* (see page 128), and in the UK as part of *The First Singles Box* (see also page 128) and as a CD single in its own right.

The group that comprised The Who by this time was by and large the group that toured the US in the summer of 2002 following the death of John Entwistle. As well and Pete and Roger it included John Bundrick on keyboards, Zak Starkey on drums, Pino Palladino on bass and Pete's brother Simon on additional guitar. (Because Palladino was committed to a Simon & Garfunkel tour, former King Crimson and ELP man Greg Lake actually plays bass on 'Real Good Looking Boy'). Starkey, of course, has been The Who's drummer of choice since 1996 and was by now widely regarded as Keith Moon's natural successor. The group that has been called The Millennium Who – or Who2 by Pete – toured extensively to great acclaim in the US in 2002 with UK dates and a Far East/Australian/Californian tour to follow in 2004 - capturing some of the spirit of the original band.

Both these new songs were recorded at Pete's Eel Pie Oceanic Studios by the River Thames at Twickenham during the winter of 2003/2004. They were performed live during show at London's Kentish Town Forum and at the Royal Albert Hall in March 2004. Whether a complete new album will be forthcoming was undecided when this book went to press.

REAL GOOD LOOKING BOY
*(Townshend/Creatore/
Peretti/Weiss)*

A CURIOUS hybrid of Elvis' ballad 'Can Help Falling In Love' (hence the credits) and an original medium pace rocker, 'Real Good Looking Boy' may lack the dynamics of classic Who but it's no slouch either, with Roger giving his all on the catchy hook line and a nice fat production that features Pete's guitar well up front. It's a morality tale in which the protagonist, having been told by his mum that he's an 'ugly' boy finds salvation in the arms of his girl whose love makes him feel he's a 'real good looking boy' after all. The inclusion of further lines from 'Can Help...' suggests the model for the good looking boy might be Elvis himself.

OLD RED WINE

TAKEN AT a slower pace than the A-side, Roger is again in fine voice on a ditty about wine. It's been suggested that the title is an allegory for John Entwistle – "Old red wine – well past its prime" – but it's an ambivalent theory. The faster coda, with the repeated line "Let it breathe", recalls The Who circa *Quadrophenia* and another fat production hints a Who-like aggression as the song draws to a close.

VIDEO/DVD

MORE THAN ANY OTHER ACTS OF THEIR ERA, THE WHO WERE RECEPTIVE to film cameras. Early managers Kit Lambert and Chris Stamp came from a film background and weren't slow to realise the promotional advantage of film, and for this reason there is good footage of The Who kicking around from the Sixties and Seventies, but certainly not enough to satiate old Who fans.

The pair's initial attraction to The Who came about largely through their appreciation of The Who's visual appeal, which they sought to enhance with lights and mayhem, and they were among the first to film performance footage of a rock band purely for promotional use.

Of course, technological advances continue, no more self-evident than in the area of video. The old battle between VHS and Beta-max is now only of limited historical interest and even seems rather innocent, as the music fan must now confront approximately nine different digital formats. (Does anyone remember Digital Tapes?) Accordingly, unless an item is not available in a commercially available digital format, video catalogue numbers are consigned to history alongside 8-Track and cassette releases.

The Complete Monterey Pop Festival

US; 3 DVD set, Criterion MON320, 2003

THE ORIGINAL MONTEREY POP MOVIE INCLUDES THE WHO PERFORMING 'My Generation' and the previously-unreleased DVD outtakes feature 'Substitute', 'Summertime Blues', and 'A Quick One (While He's Away)'. All from June 18, 1967.

The Rolling Stones
Rock And Roll Circus

US: VHS ABKCO 38781-1003-3, 1996

THIS LEGENDARY UNRELEASED TELEVISION SPECIAL, FILMED **DECEMBER 10 & 11,** 1968 was well worth the 28-year wait, if not for the scorching version of 'A Quick One While He's Away' – one of the most arresting aspects of the show. Arresting enough to believe the myth that the Stones quashed the film's release because The Who's performance upstaged the big boys.

Woodstock:
The Director's Cut

US: Warner Brothers 13549

Woodstock Diaries

UK: Warner Brothers 231121

BETWEEN THESE TWO RELEASES, **'WE'RE NOT GONNA TAKE IT', 'SUMMERTIME** Blues', and 'My Generation' are represented from The Who's appearance at the legendary August 1969 festival they ended up hating. What about a DVD release of what survives of the whole set?

Live At The Isle Of Wight
Festival 1970

UK: Warner Music 0630-14360-2 | US: Image Entertainment ID4698ERDVD

BECAUSE THE *LIVE AT LEEDS* CONCERT WASN'T FILMED, THEN THIS WILL HAVE to do, if only to see John Entwistle, even more immovable than usual, crammed into a skeleton suit that was apparently a size too small. The band's overall performance is very good indeed, and this is as close as we can get to seeing the classic Who hitting its stride as the world's greatest live rock band. Entwistle later claimed that The Who sounded best during the 1975 or 1976 period, but this lengthy show makes a strong case that 1970 was of a superior vintage.

The Old Grey Whistle Test Vol. 2

UK: BBC Worldwide BBCDVD 1279, 2003

THE WHO PERFUNCTORILY PERFORM 'RELAY' FROM JANUARY 1973.

Tommy The Movie

US: Columbia 10015, 2002

Quadrophenia

UK: Universal DVD 051 835 2, 1999 | US: Rhino R2 976624, 2001

The Kids Are Alright

EU: BMG 74321 100878, 2004 | US: Pioneer 12116;
Pioneer 12103 Deluxe Edition, 2003;
UK: DVD Sanctuary SUE 3050, VHS Sanctuary SUE 3750

AN ESSENTIAL UPGRADED **DVD** THAT RESTORES THE ORIGINAL UNEDITED cinema print, at the correct speed with a 5.1 stereo audio track.

This first-rate, 100 minute biopic – among the apex of rock on celluloid – appeared as an unwitting tribute to Keith Moon when first issued in 1979. Directed with genuine affection by US fan Jeff Stein, this exhilarating, non-chronologically assembled documentary includes live and lip-synched footage and interviews stretching back to 1964, concluding with 'Won't Get

Fooled Again' from a specially filmed performance at Shepperton Studios in 1978, which turned out to be Moon's last stand. Highlights include non-split screen footage from Woodstock ('Pinball Wizard', 'Sparks' and 'See Me, Feel Me') though the camera focuses primarily on Roger to the detriment of the rest of the band, 'A Quick One' from *The Rolling Stones' Rock & Roll Circus*, and spectacular footage of the band smashing their equipment, notably the (literally) explosive opening sequence from *The Smothers Brothers Comedy Hour* (The Who's US TV debut) in 1967.

Also worth mentioning are some amusing and insightful interviews with Pete stretching back to 1965 and the non-performance B&W promotional film made for 'Happy Jack' in 1966. Whoever suggested that Queen's 'Bohemian Rhapsody' was 'the first ever pop video' needs to get their facts straight.

The Kids Are Alright is the definitive rock documentary, essential not only to Who fans but lovers of music in general.

The Who Rocks America 1982

UK VHS: CBS/FOX 6234-50, 1984

A COMPLETE CONCERT BY THE WHO WITH KENNEY JONES ON DRUMS AND Tim Gorman on keyboards filmed not in America as the title implies but at Toronto's Maple Leaf Garden on December 17, 1982, during the band's first 'farewell tour' of North America. By anyone else's standards The Who were still a great rock band but compared to their sprightly early days, they were going through the motions by this time, banging out the hits and throwing in a few new songs to keep the record company happy. Pete doesn't so much look bored as resigned, and reproducing the agile athleticism of old seems now to be a great effort. Only Roger retains the enthusiasm of old, not that John *ever* betrayed his emotions on stage. Not available on DVD to date.

Who's Better Who's Best

UK VHS: Channel 5 CFV 05562, 1988

A VIDEO COLLECTION OF FOOTAGE, LIVE AND LIP-SYNCHED, OF THE WHO performing their best-known songs, marred by the inclusion of several clips that already appeared in *The Kids Are Alright*. Not essential, although clips of 'The Kids Are Alright' (promo film, 1966), 'I Can See For Miles' (The Smothers Brothers, 1967) and the opening 'My Generation' (*Beat Club*, 1967) are worth the price of admission. The clips for 'I'm Free' (London Coliseum, 1969) and 'Magic Bus' (Holland, 1973) are unavailable elsewhere while the laser disc version features 'Relay' from *The Russell Harty Show* (1973) which is also otherwise unobtainable.

Live Tommy

UK VHS: CMV Enterprises 49028 2, 1989

A **COMPLETE CONCERT FROM THE 1989 25TH ANNIVERSARY TOUR FILMED AT** the Universal Amphitheater in Los Angeles on August 24. This particular show was a charity event in which several guest artists took part in *Tommy*, which occupies the entire first half of the video. Guests include Elton John, Phil Collins, Steve Winwood, Patti Labelle, and Billy Idol. During the second half, the much augmented Who band run through a selection of hits. For the enthusiast only and not available (to date) on DVD.

30 Years Of Maximum R&B Live

UK: Polydor 2003 | US: MCA 088 111 066-9, 2001

A **N EXCELLENT COMPANION TO *THE KIDS ARE ALRIGHT* AND THE WHO'S BOX SET,** *30 Years of Maximum R&B* presents two and a half hours of genuine live performances by The Who arranged chronologically and punctuated by 1994 interviews with Pete, Roger and John in which they talk about The Who's career, with particular emphasis on the development of their stage career. Considering the amount of footage already on Kids, producer Nick Ryle did an outstanding job researching all this 'new' footage, none of which was on Kids or had been available commercially prior to this release.

Among the many highlights are two numbers from the Isle Of Wight set in 1970 ('Young Man Blues' and 'I Don't Even Know Myself'), and four from The Who's first massive open air gig at Charlton Football Ground in 1974 ('Substitute', 'Drowned', 'Bell Boy' and 'My Generation').

The first 90 minutes feature The Who with Keith Moon (seen on his best form during a snappy 'Happy Jack' from the London Coliseum in 1969); thereafter it's Kenney Jones on drums and, at the conclusion, The Who plus the touring ensemble that gathered for their 1989 25th anniversary tour. The differences between the original Who and the post-Moon outfits are most pronounced; definitive proof indeed that Keith's drums were an essential ingredient in The Who's sound, a far more crucial factor than the role played by any other drummer of his or subsequent generations.

Also included in the package are excellent liner notes by John Atkins, including precise details about the origins of the clips. After *The Kids Are Alright*, this is the essential DVD to own for any Who fan.

Classic Albums: The Who - Who's Next

UK: ILC DVD2011, US: Image Entertainment ID9075SERDVD, 1999

A WORTHWHILE LOOK INTO THE MAKING OF *WHO'S NEXT* ALTHOUGH THERE isn't enough discussion on *Lifehouse* and the associated Young Vic experimental concerts. More like a snack than the full course meal, to borrow a metaphor, this is ultimately frustrating because the harder questions were not asked.

The Who: The Vegas Job Live In Vegas

UK: United Energy Entertainment DVDL001D, 2003

O NLY THE WHO COULD GET ENTANGLED IN ONE OF THE BIGGEST INTERNET scams ever. A reunion concert in Vegas was supposed to go out around the world via the Internet to an eagerly waiting audience of millions. It didn't work out that way and, millions of dollars later all the technology could not broadcast anything beyond the four walls of the venue itself.

The Who & Special Guests

Live At The Royal Albert Hall

US: Image Entertainment ID0659MYDVD, 2001

SEE *LIVE AT THE ROYAL ALBERT HALL* FOR GUESTS AND TRACK LISTING.

The Concert For New York City

US: CMV C2D 54295, 2001

THE MADISON SQUARE GARDEN SHOW, PRESENTED OCTOBER 20, 2001 as New York's response to "9/11" as the Twin Tower terrorist attacks are now universally known. Whatever the politics involved, Pete's comments were sincere and compassionate in showing concern for his American audience. The Who steal the show, performing 'Who Are You', 'Baba O'Riley', 'Behind Blue Eyes' and 'Won't Get Fooled Again'.

The Who Special EP

UK: DTS DVD6068X, 2002

FROM *BEAT CLUB* GERMAN TV: 'SEE ME FEEL ME' (1969), 'I'M A BOY' (1966) and 'Pinball Wizard' (1969). A fourth track, 'I'm Free' (1969) is listed but is not included.

BETWEEN 2001 AND 2003 VARIOUS OTHER GERMAN *BEAT CLUB* DVDs WERE released featuring a few isolated performances by The Who (amongst others) recorded between 1966 and 1969.

Index